ISSUES THAT CONCERN YOU

Dress Codes in Schools

Cynthia A. Bily, *Book Editor*

GREENHAVEN PRESS
A part of Gale, Cengage Learning

Detroit • New York • San Francisco • New Haven, Conn • Waterville, Maine • London

Elizabeth Des Chenes, *Director, Content Strategy*
Cynthia Sanner, *Publisher*
Douglas Dentino, *Manager, New Product*

For more information, contact:
Greenhaven Press
27500 Drake Rd.
Farmington Hills, MI 48331-3535
Or you can visit our Internet site at gale.cengage.com

Articles in Greenhaven Press anthologies are often edited for length to meet page require-ments. In addition, original titles of these works are changed to clearly present the main thesis and to explicitly indicate the author's opinion. Every effort is made to ensure that Greenhaven Press accurately reflects the original intent of the authors. Every effort has been made to trace the owners of copyrighted material.

Cover image © Steve Woods/Shutterstock.com.

LIBRARY OF CONGRESS CATALOGING-IN-PUBLICATION DATA

Dress codes in schools (2014)
   Dress codes in schools / Cynthia A. Bily, book editor.
       pages cm. -- (Issues that concern you)
   Summary: "Issues That Concern You: Dress Codes in Schools: This series provides readers with information on topics of current interest. Focusing on important social issues, each anthology examines its subject in a variety of ways, from personal accounts to factual articles"-- Provided by publisher.
   Includes bibliographical references and index.
   ISBN 978-0-7377-6930-2 (hardback)
   1. Students--Clothing--United States--Juvenile literature. 2. Students--United States--Uniforms--Juvenile literature. 3. Dress codes--United States--Juvenile literature. I. Bily, Cynthia A., editor of compilation. II. Title.
   LB3024.D744 2014
   371.5'1--dc23
                                                                          2013043019

Printed in the United States of America
1 2 3 4 5 6 7 18 17 16 15 14

CONTENTS

"This remarkable progress that you have shown in your school as a result of your school uniform policy, making it safer, more disciplined, orderly, creates teachers who focus on teaching and students who focus on their job of learning."

—President Bill Clinton, speech at Jackie Robinson Academy, Long Beach, California, February 24, 1996

After President Bill Clinton called for more schools to adopt required uniforms in 1996, the US Department of Education sent a *Manual on School Uniforms* to every school district in the country. The manual pointed to several potential benefits of school uniforms—including the prevention of violence, especially gang violence, an increase in discipline, and enhanced learning—and encouraged districts to make school uniforms a part of their plans to improve school quality. Since that time, however, the research on the effectiveness of uniforms and less restrictive dress codes has failed to show clear benefits. While many administrators, teachers, parents, and even students believe that their dress codes make students and staff behave more formally or feel more like a community, the data that have been gathered by experts do not show significant improvements in safety, discipline, or learning.

Many parents favor school uniforms because uniforms can save them money, especially in districts where students are eager to have the latest fashions. Teachers who favor uniforms say that the policies save them the headaches that come from using valuable class time to enforce less specific dress codes, and they say that uniforms keep students from using clothing to establish social and class-based hierarchies. If everyone dresses the same way, they argue, everyone is more likely to be treated the same way. Some students, after they have lived with a dress code or uniform for a while, come to agree that not having to worry about what to wear saves them time and anxiety.

President Bill Clinton speaks at a school in Moravia, California, in 1996. He endorsed the suburban Los Angeles city's efforts to combat teen crime through the use of curfews and school uniforms.

But many students find their schools' dress codes and uniform policies frustrating and demeaning, and the newspapers are filled with stories of students who defied their school rules. Some students find themselves in trouble for trying to express themselves. Hannah Adams, a middle school student in South

Carolina, was suspended in 2012 for dying some of her hair bright red, and in 2013 Ariel Davila was suspended from her Colorado middle school for dying her hair blue. One hundred students in a Mississippi school were suspended on the first day of school in 2012 because they wore neon-colored shoes that violated their school's policy forbidding gang-related clothing. And that same year, when Danielle O'Neal was suspended from her North Carolina middle school for having her shirt untucked, her principal told a reporter for *Compass News 360°*, "Her shirttail was a good four or five inches below her sweater all the way around. She's a good kid, but my job is to make sure students follow our school's Code of Conduct."

While expressing personal style is important to many students, others find that dress codes get in the way of expressing issues that are important to them. Two elementary school girls in Texas, whose father was paralyzed while fighting in Afghanistan, were disciplined for wearing T-shirts with the logo of a group called Homes for Our Troops; the shirts violated the parts of their school dress code that forbid collarless shirts and shirts with logos. About twenty students in Ohio were ordered to remove shirts with rainbow logos that supported gay rights. And when Rheanne Sargent, another South Carolina student, was suspended for dying her hair pink to support National Breast Cancer Awareness Month, her mother took Rheanne's side and told an interviewer for local TV station WYFF, "If the child wants . . . to show that they're supporting something . . . I believe, yeah, they should make an exception."

In each of these cases, students and school administrators are at odds, and parents and teachers often do not know which side to support. Everyone agrees that schools must provide a safe and nurturing environment for children so that they can learn. How to balance academic learning with learning to stand up for oneself and express important ideas is an issue that has always proved difficult for schools. School administrators have many constituents to please, and as in the case of dress codes, they must make decisions before evidence can tell them conclusively which path is best. Matt Buesing, a school uniform consultant in New Jersey, warned in the *School Administrator* magazine that "the most successful school uniform policies are not implemented in isolation, but rather as part of a larger school reform effort."

These issues about school dress codes—and the best ways to work through them—are addressed by the authors of the viewpoints in *Issues That Concern You: Dress Codes in Schools*. In addition, the volume contains several appendixes to help the reader understand and explore the topic, including a thorough bibliography and a list of organizations to contact for further information. The appendix titled "What You Should Know About Dress Codes in Schools" offers facts about how different groups of people think about dress codes and what the courts have said about them. The appendix "What You Should Do About Dress Codes in Schools" offers tips for young people interested in learning more about these issues and talking effectively about them. With all these features, *Issues That Concern You: Dress Codes in Schools* provides an excellent resource for everyone interested in this issue.

ONE

Dress Codes Are Intended to Help Students Learn

Marian Wilde

> In the following viewpoint Marian Wilde gives an over-
> view of the issues surrounding dress codes and school
> uniforms and the arguments frequently raised in sup-
> port of and in opposition to them. It is important for
> students and parents to read school dress policies care-
> fully, she explains, to understand a student's rights and
> responsibilities. The research about the effectiveness of
> school dress codes is inconclusive, she states, but the
> belief that these codes can enhance student learning
> and safety continues. Wilde is a frequent contributor to
> the GreatSchools website, as well as the mother of two
> school-age children.

For the past decade, schools, parents and students have clashed over the issue of regulating student attire. In 2007, cases involving an anti–[President George W.] Bush T-shirt in Vermont, an anti-gay T-shirt in San Diego and Tigger socks in Napa, California, made their way through the courts, causing many to wonder whether this debate will ever be resolved.

Meanwhile, researchers are divided over how much of an impact—if any—dress policies have upon student learning. A 2004 book makes the case that uniforms do not improve school safety or academic discipline. A 2005 study, on the other hand, indicates that in some Ohio high schools uniforms may have improved graduation and attendance rates, although no improvements were observed in academic performance.

Why Have Uniforms?

In the 1980s, public schools were often compared unfavorably to Catholic schools. Noting the perceived benefit that uniforms conferred upon Catholic schools, some public schools decided to adopt a school uniform policy.

President [Bill] Clinton provided momentum to the school uniform movement when he said in his 1996 State of the Union speech, "If it means teenagers will stop killing each other over designer jackets, then our public schools should be able to require their students to wear school uniforms."

According to proponents, school uniforms:

- Help prevent gangs from forming on campus
- Encourage discipline
- Help students resist peer pressure to buy trendy clothes
- Help identify intruders in the school
- Diminish economic and social barriers between students
- Increase a sense of belonging and school pride
- Improve attendance

Opponents contend that school uniforms:

- Violate a student's right to freedom of expression
- Are simply a Band-Aid on the issue of school violence
- Make students a target for bullies from other schools
- Are a financial burden for poor families
- Are an unfair additional expense for parents who pay taxes for a free public education
- Are difficult to enforce in public schools

Schools and districts vary widely in how closely they adhere to the concept of uniformity.

In the 1980s public schools were often compared unfavorably with Catholic schools. Noting the perceived benefits that uniforms seemed to bestow on Catholic schools, some public schools decided to adopt uniforms, too.

What Is a Dress Code?

Generally, dress codes are much less restrictive than uniform policies. Sometimes, however, dress codes are nearly as strict, as in the case of a middle school in Napa, California. This particular school's dress code required students to wear solid colors and banned images or logos on clothes. When a student was sent to detention for wearing socks adorned with the image of Winnie-the-Pooh's friend Tigger, the girl's family sued the school district for violating her freedom of speech. In August of 2007, the district announced it would relax its dress code—for the time being—to allow images and fabrics other than solid colors. The district superintendent, while admitting that banning images on clothes raises concerns about the restriction of political and religious speech, announced his intention to move soon toward implementing uniforms in the district.

Uniforms are certainly easier for administrators to enforce than dress codes. Consider two recent examples of students challenging dress codes through the courts.

In June of 2007, the United States Supreme Court upheld a lower court's decision affirming a Vermont student's right to wear a T-shirt depicting President Bush surrounded by drug and alcohol images. The school had suspended the student, not for the anti-Bush political statement, but for violating a dress code that prohibits drug and alcohol images. The courts, however, disagreed with the school and found that, because the images referred to Bush's alleged past use of cocaine and alcohol, they were protected as free political expression.

In March of 2007, the Supreme Court "vacated" or set aside the decision of a lower court upholding a San Diego high school's suspension of a student for wearing an anti-gay T-shirt. The school argued that the T-shirt was hateful and inflammatory. The Supreme Court's action essentially struck down the school's argument and upheld the student's right to free speech.

In both of these cases, the schools' attempts to protect students from drug and alcohol images or hateful speech were reversed in favor of free speech. To clarify the matter somewhat, the Supreme Court ruled in June of 2007 in favor of a school in Alaska that had suspended a student for displaying a banner reading "Bong Hits 4 Jesus." The court ruled that the reference to drugs in this case had no political message and could indeed be seen as advocating drug use.

Check with your school to see what the dress code is, as they can be fairly specific. In Tulsa, Oklahoma, for example, the dress code prohibits:

- Decorations (including tattoos) that are symbols, mottoes, words or acronyms that convey crude, vulgar, profane, violent, gang-related, sexually explicit or suggestive messages

- Large or baggy clothes (this prohibition can be used to keep students from excessive "sagging")
- Holes in clothes
- Scarves, curlers, bandanas or sweatbands inside of school buildings (exceptions are made for religious attire)
- Visible undergarments
- Strapless garments
- Bare midriffs, immodestly low-cut necklines or bare backs
- Tights, leggings, bike shorts, swim suits or pajamas as outerwear
- Visible piercings, except in the ear
- Dog collars, tongue rings and studs, wallet chains, large hair picks, or chains that connect one part of the body to another

What Is a Uniform?

One school might require white button-down shirts and ties for boys, pleated skirts for girls and blazers adorned with the school logo for all. Another school may simply require that all shirts have collars.

In Toledo, Ohio, elementary school students have a limited palette of colors that they can wear: white, light blue, dark blue or yellow on the top half and dark blue, navy, khaki or tan on the bottom half.

Toledo girls are allowed a fairly wide range of dress items, however: blouses, polo shirts with collars, turtlenecks, skirts, jumpers, slacks, and knee-length shorts and skirts. Boys have almost as many choices: dress shirts, turtlenecks, polo or button-down shirts, pants or knee-length shorts.

When Toledo students reach junior high, they are treated to one more color choice: maroon.

What Research Says About School Uniforms

Virginia Draa, assistant professor at Youngstown State University, reviewed attendance, graduation and proficiency pass rates at 64 public high schools in Ohio. Her final analysis surprised her: "I really went into this thinking uniforms don't make a difference,

Dress Code Requirements Are Consistent

Since the beginning of the twenty-first century, the proportion of American public schools that enforce strict dress codes has remained relatively stable, at a little more than half.

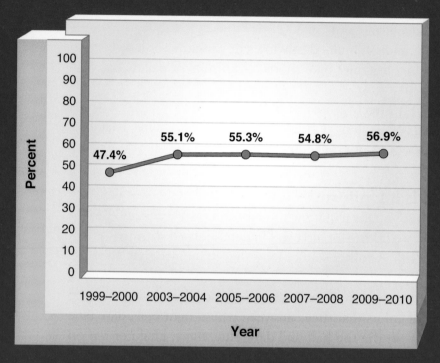

Taken from: US Department of Education, Institute of Education Sciences, National Center for Education Statistics. "Indicators of School Crime and Safety: 2011," http://nces.ed.gov/programs/crimeindicators/crimeindicators2011/tables/table_20_1.asp.

but I came away seeing that they do. At least at these schools, they do. I was absolutely floored."

Draa's study concluded that those schools with uniform policies improved in attendance, graduation and suspension rates. She was unable to connect uniforms with academic improvement because of such complicating factors as changing instructional methods and curriculum.

University of Missouri assistant professor David Brunsma reached a different conclusion. In his 2004 book, *The School*

Uniform Movement and What It Tells Us About American Education: A Symbolic Crusade, Brunsma reviewed past studies on the effect of uniforms on academic performance. He also conducted his own analysis of two enormous databases, the 1988 National Educational Longitudinal Study and the 1998 Early Childhood Longitudinal Study. Brunsma concluded that there is no positive correlation between uniforms and school safety or academic achievement.

Meanwhile, the movement toward uniforms in public schools has spread to about a quarter of all elementary schools. Experts say that the number of middle and high schools with uniforms is about half the number of elementary schools. If uniforms are intended to curb school violence and improve academics, why are they not more prevalent in middle and high schools, where these goals are just as important as in elementary schools? Because, says Brunsma, "It's desperately much more difficult to implement uniforms in high schools, and even middle schools, for student resistance is much, much higher. In fact, most of the litigation resulting from uniforms has been located at levels of K–12 [kindergarten through grade twelve] that are higher than elementary schools. Of course, this uniform debate is also one regarding whether children have rights, too!"

A new trend is the mounting pressure to establish dress codes for teachers. Apparently the same casual mind-set toward revealing outfits is cropping up in the ranks of our teachers.

The debate over uniforms in public schools encompasses many larger issues than simply what children should wear to school. It touches on issues of school improvement, freedom of expression and the "culture wars." It's no wonder the debate rages on.

TWO

Dress Codes Help Set the Proper Tone in School

Doreen Umutesi

In the following viewpoint journalist Doreen Umutesi presents the argument—widely accepted in Africa, where Umutesi lives and works—that wearing school uniforms helps keep students safe. The uniform, according to school administrators quoted in the viewpoint, makes it easy for staff to know instantly whether a person on school grounds belongs there. Although buying the uniforms can be difficult for some poor families, they argue, wearing the uniforms teaches students discipline and respect. Umutesi is a features writer and photographer for the *New Times*, a major daily newspaper in the central African nation of Rwanda.

When Elizabeth Kaitesi was in high school, it was unthinkable for a student to move around during school time when not wearing school uniform. Today, she looks on in astonishment as students change into casual wear, with the girls into their "adorable" and tight-fitting pants, as soon as they step out of the school gate. The habit is common among secondary school students.

Some students leave home in the morning with casual clothes, which they change into after school. Educationists argue that this compromises the security and identity of students in case of a problem. School uniform helps with identification of students in case of an emergency. But it also has a link to discipline and academic performance, according to academic research.

Last year [2012], the Ministry of Education [of Rwanda] gave directives on regulation of school uniforms, which schools are supposed to implement. The ministry directed that each student must wear uniform to and from school to ensure safety and easy identification of students.

The requirement for students to wear school uniform is not only for safety and identification but a requirement for every student.

In Africa school uniforms are very important because they distinguish students from other people.

Dress Codes and School District Image

In a 2011 survey of active American school board members in districts with uniform or dress code policies, most agreed that the policies helped create a positive image for the district.

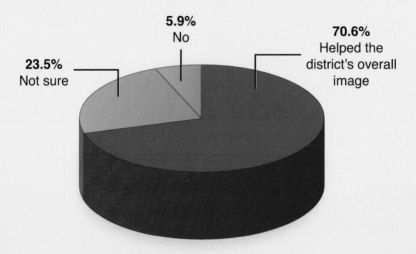

5.9%
No

23.5%
Not sure

70.6%
Helped the district's overall image

Taken from: 2011 Classroom School Uniforms. "Survey, Executive Summary & Key Findings," July 25, 2011. www.classroomuniforms.com.

John Rutayisire, the director-general of Rwanda Education Board (Reb), echoes the importance of the school uniform policy which schools must adhere to.

"It's a policy for all primary and secondary school going students to have a uniform. But the choice and colour of uniform is up to individual schools," Rutayisire emphasises.

He acknowledges that there have been challenges in implementing this policy.

"One of the challenges is in the nine-year basic education schools where the government pays fees for everyone, but does not pay for the uniforms. The uniform is supposed to be paid for by the parents or guardians. But some of these parents or guardians are too poor to afford and hence take long to buy the uniforms for their children," Rutayisire reveals.

Schools Speak Out

According to Sam Nkurunziza, the Headmaster of Kagarama Secondary School in Kicukiro district, uniform is very important because it distinguishes students from other people.

"Although we have never encountered a problem where a student can't afford, if a student is not dressed in proper uniform, he or she will not enter the school premises," Nkurunziza reveals. He further adds that besides sportswear, no other kind of wear is allowed in school apart from the uniform.

"This is a boarding school, but we don't allow casual wear on school campus and even when students are going back home or reporting back to school, we insist they put on a proper school uniform," he emphasises.

Ivan Mbaraga, a teacher at Green Hills Academy, concurs. He says uniform is important both in school and outside school.

"The image of a student in uniform and one without a uniform is totally different. A uniform's main importance is for identity and for the student to look smart."

According to Green Hills standards, being smart requires fully dressing up in the authorised school uniform.

He further warns that if a uniform is misused, it gives a bad image and compromises the purpose and objective of a school uniform. Green Hills is one of the best schools with strict rules on school uniform and discipline.

Mbaraga says the school doesn't allow students to come to school unless they are dressed in uniform. However, for certain days, like if students have Physical Education, they come dressed in sportswear.

"We have to explain to these students why it's bad to abuse the school uniform like walking with their shirts hanging out or the tie loosened. We can do this as teachers, parents and the communities at large to promote smartness of Rwandan students," Mbaraga advises.

Parents Speak Out

Although some schools have been blamed for the inappropriate dress code of students, fingers are also pointing at the parents.

Patricia Garuka Mugume, a mother of three, advises fellow parents to play a role in grooming children to embrace discipline and smartness.

"If I see a student who is dressed up inappropriately, it makes me think that the parent is not paying proper attention to the child and how he dresses," Mugume says.

She calls for more involvement of parents in proper grooming of children.

"I have done this with my daughter in nursery. She already knows that her uniform is supposed to be organised in a certain way in terms of presentation. This is the discipline they get when they are still young which will help them when they grow up," Garuka reveals.

She also says the uniform dress code in schools encourages and makes students relate as equals.

"With the same uniform, we won't have students saying, 'you have this I don't have that'. If the students are dressed in school uniform, it helps them focus on studies without getting distracted on whether they are dressed better than their colleagues," Garuka observes.

Other parents agree with Garuka's view.

"We are supposed to shape morals of children. Dressing is part of the whole morality process. Allowing a child to wear unauthorised school wear will send the wrong message. Students will think they can wear what they like," argues a parent.

Irene Umutoni, a mother of five, believes in schools that are strict on uniform.

"The uniform makes students look decent and neat. Casual wear brings out an allure of indecency in a school setting. Schools have to be conscious of the kind of image they portray to the public," says Umutoni.

Gloria Ngabire, a teacher, echoes the view. "They look more of students when they wear uniform," Ngabire argues.

THREE

Dress Codes Make Schools Safer

National School Safety and Security Services

> In the following viewpoint the author argues that school policies restricting what students may wear and what kinds of book bags they may carry can make schools safer. These policies, the author contends, improve the overall climate of a school, and this in turn makes it less likely that crimes will occur there. Restrictions on student dress and expression during school hours—in the name of safety—are more than balanced out by the freedom to choose their own wardrobes the rest of the day, the author concludes. The viewpoint was published by National School Safety and Security Services, a consulting firm specializing in school safety, emergency preparedness, and violence-prevention training.

National School Safety and Security Services receives a number of inquiries regarding the issue of school uniforms, dress codes, book bag control, and their role in improving school safety and security. Although we believe that no single strategy is a panacea for improving school safety, we do believe that school uniforms, dress codes, and book bag control can contribute toward improving the school climate. School climate, of course, can play a significant role in reducing security threats and improving school safety.

Uniforms and Dress Codes

School officials have a responsibility to provide a safe, secure, and productive learning environment. Dress and appearance play a role in doing so. Although we do not support violating the law, including the legal rights of others, we do believe that properly implemented policies and strategies around dress and appearance are within the realm of reasonable actions which can be taken by school officials to promote a positive school climate.

Dress codes and uniforms can help reduce the potential for conflict by:

- Reducing conflict stemming from socio-economic status, i.e., conflicts stemming from comments and personal attacks about who has better clothing and so on.
- Reducing ways in which gang members can identify themselves which, in essence, is a form of intimidation and creates fear.
- Reduces the risk of students being robbed to and from school, or for that matter in school, of expensive clothing, jewelry, etc.
- In the case of uniforms, could help school administrators identify non-students, trespassers, and other visitors in the hallways who stand out in the crowd.

These are general observations and, of course, there are exceptions. For example, one group of students told us that although they had uniforms, the school policy did not specify specific types of uniforms, so some students wore very expensive dark pants and light shirts, while others wore less expensive ones, and the status reduction argument was thus moot. Of course, there are also many ways for gang members to identify themselves in addition to dress, too, so uniforms do not eliminate gangs or all of their ways to identify. Still, the fact that there are some glitches and ways to beat the system should not shoot down the entire concept.

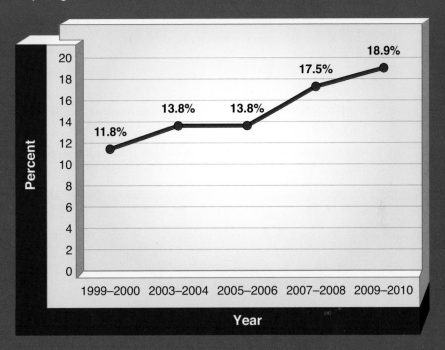

More Schools Require Uniforms

Since the turn of the century, the percentage of public schools requiring students to wear uniforms has increased.

Percent vs. Year

- 1999–2000: 11.8%
- 2003–2004: 13.8%
- 2005–2006: 13.8%
- 2007–2008: 17.5%
- 2009–2010: 18.9%

Taken from: US Department of Education, Institute of Education Sciences, National Center for Education Statistics. "Indicators of School Crime and Safety." http://nces.ed.gov/programs/crimeindicators/crimindicators2011/tables /table_20_1.asp.

Student and parent input should be received on the front-end of implementing such policies, especially school uniforms. Anecdotal information suggests that such involvement reduces non-compliance and increases ownership into the program. Ironically, once implemented, many students and staff are pleased with uniforms, for example, and parents are also pleased with the idea that they are often cheaper than common popular clothing, plus they do not have the hassle with their children each day of dealing with "what to wear" to school.

Do dress codes and uniforms violate freedom of expression opportunities? We think that this argument is quite weak.

Students are free to dress as they and their parents choose during non-school hours. They also need to realize that dress codes and uniforms are a reality of the workplace in the adult world including in professional offices, retail and food stores, delivery services, government offices and service providers such as post offices, public safety employers, and so on.

Kenneth Trump, president of the Cleveland chapter of National School Safety and Security Services, addresses school officials around the country on how school policies restricting what students may wear and what kinds of book bags they may carry can make their schools safer.

Although we would question whether uniforms or dress codes alone are responsible for major school crime reductions, our anecdotal information, experiences, and observations in the field suggest that they do improve school climate.

Book Bags

Should schools go to clear or see-through book bags? Should they eliminate book bags?

We have no opposition to clear book bags or the banning of book bags in halls and classrooms, but we do not believe that these strategies, in themselves, will *guarantee* that weapons will not make it into the school or classroom. Naturally, someone could still carry weapons on his or her person, and we acknowledge this up front. However, it does *reduce risks* by taking away one method for carrying them around the school all day.

More importantly, requiring students to leave book bags in their lockers during the school day reduces the risks of conflicts arising from hallway horseplay, bumping of other students with book bags, and similar dynamics that often lead to fights and altercations, including those where weapons may be used. This requirement, in our opinion, balances out legitimate needs to have book bags for carrying large numbers of books home while still reducing the potential for conflicts, especially in schools with tight hallways and stairwells. It also teaches students to plan ahead several periods—and an ability to plan is a necessity for survival in the adult business and personal worlds!

FOUR

Dress Codes May Not Make Schools Safer

Julian Tanner

In the following viewpoint Julian Tanner describes the intensified security measures that schools in the United States and Canada have taken since the school shooting at Columbine High School in Colorado in 1999. Many schools have begun to require uniforms in the hopes that the policies would reduce gang activity and increase safety in schools. Emphasis on what students wear is misguided, he concludes, because it has not been shown to increase safety and because it draws administrators' focus away from more important concerns. Tanner is a professor of sociology at the University of Toronto; he studies the interests and activities of young people.

It is now over ten years since the shootings at Columbine High School in April 1999. While Columbine was not the first school shooting in the United States, or the last, it remains the most important. For many people, but especially for parents, the name 'Columbine' has become a one-word summation of fears and concerns about the condition of modern youth. In particular—and not surprisingly—the events in Columbine have concentrated public attention on school safety and school-based crime.

On the face of it, these concerns are well justified. Research that Scot Wortley and I conducted in Toronto several years ago confirms that school is a significant site of student victimization, though most of the incidents described to us did not involve serious violence. American research also shows that neighbourhoods, businesses, and shopping malls bordering high schools experience more crime than their more isolated counterparts. This research also shows that the journey to and (particularly) from school affords more opportunities for—and fewer constraints against—crime than the schools themselves. Other American research indicates that schools are not the principal places where violence by or against adolescents occurs. Such incidents are more likely to take place in or near the victim's home or in the community than in the school itself. By any reasonable standard, schools themselves are, as they have always been, relatively safe places for young people.

Needless to say, this is not how schools are commonly viewed. In the wake of Columbine, most school boards in North America have embarked upon various safe school and anti-bullying policies and programs, in response to real public anxiety about safety in schools. Many of these initiatives have never been properly evaluated; of those that have, some have been found to be ineffective and others have been found to produce effects that were presumably unintended. . . .

School Uniforms: Initial Optimism

When I was growing up and going to school in England, I was required to wear a uniform. I hated it: hated the uniform, hated the rule. The official and often-repeated justification for the policy was an egalitarian one: requiring pupils to wear uniforms masked otherwise invidious class and status distinctions among them.

Apparently, similar motivations once informed school uniform policies where they existed in North America. However, the post-Columbine rationale for school uniforms is much more likely to emphasize safety and disciplinary issues. As explained to me by one high school principal several years ago (and, I suspect, probably accepted by many in the teaching profession as common knowledge), school uniforms make it easier for school personnel to spot unwanted intruders in the hallways and prevent the importation of some of the most obvious signs and symbols of gang culture into the school setting.

Findings from Southern California provided early support for claims about the positive effects of school uniforms. The Long Beach School District was one of the first large school boards in North America to introduce a mandatory uniform policy. The initiative attracted a large amount of media attention—even more when statistics were published showing that the incidents of school crime declined between the 1994–1995 and 1995–1996 school years, immediately after the implementation of the uniform policy.

However, more recent and better designed longitudinal research, also from the United States, has punctured these claims. In a large, national survey, [David L.] Brunsma and [Kerry A.] Rockquemore report that, when other factors were taken into account, school uniforms had no impact upon substance use (cigarettes, alcohol, and marijuana), school attendance, or behavioural problems (in-school suspensions for skipping classes and getting into trouble). Intriguingly, they also report that a uniform policy seems to have a suppressive effect upon educational attainment. They proffer no explanation for this important reversal of the usual argument about the benefits of school uniforms. Perhaps it is because, as in the case of my own school days, young people object to a uniform policy, and that objection translates into a weakened commitment to schooling.

Certainly, there was resistance to the uniform policy in Long Beach. Emanating, in part, from the ranks of high school students, it resulted in high schools (as opposed to elementary and middle schools) becoming exempt from the policy. Ironically, this created a situation in which a policy conceived primarily as a school-based anti-gang initiative was never applied to older students, among whom gang activity might reasonably have been expected to be most prevalent.

Since the Columbine school shootings (pictured) on April 20, 1999, many schools have begun to require students to wear uniforms in the hope of increasing safety.

How might we explain the original, optimistic findings from Long Beach, California? Brunsma and Rockquemore suggest that school uniforms were, in fact, but one part of a larger package of reforms introduced by the school board. Other 'big ticket' items included curriculum reform and a reconsideration of pedagogical strategies. Brunsma and Rockquemore suggest that while uniforms received all the attention, credit for the improvements in student behaviour belonged to those other, considerably more substantive, changes. . . .

Good Schools Are Safer Schools

Generally speaking, the features that make schools good ones (as opposed to poor or mediocre ones) are the same features that

In a 2000 phone survey of 755 school principals, conducted by the National Association of Elementary School Principals (NAESP), 62 percent reported that they believe requiring school uniforms helped make schools safer.

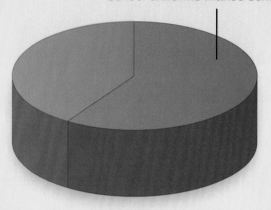

62%
Principals believe requiring school uniforms makes schools safer

Taken from: NAESP. "Survey of School Principals Reports Positive Effects of School Uniforms," July 2000.

serve to prevent or reduce crime and other disruptive behaviour at school in the first place. Schools that are able to elicit the support and commitment of the student body as a whole (and not just the academically talented) are less likely to become sites of crime than schools that fail in this regard. For instance, schools that encourage a love of learning and minimize a sense of failure among students are, at the same time, decreasing the risks of criminal behaviour. On the other hand, deviance of all sorts is encouraged by the absence of clear rules about appropriate behaviour in school or the inconsistent enforcement of rules.

Early findings from the Canadian Longitudinal Survey of Children and Youth support the conclusion that schools can modify student behaviour and reduce the incidence of violence.

Collecting information from students between ages 12 and 13, and then again two years later, when they were 14 or 15, [Jane B.] Sprott finds that supportive classrooms (and teachers that provide that support) have a reductive effect upon levels of aggression and violence; she also finds that classrooms that emphasize academic study (and the teachers who provide that focus) have a similar effect on property offences.

In our rush to assuage public fears based on a relatively few dramatic incidents of school violence, we run the risk of ignoring well-established educational strategies that improve student behaviour in favour of panaceas that are not only unproven, but may in fact have unintended and negative consequences.

FIVE

At Schools with Dress Codes, Sudents Find Ways to Express Themselves

Xazmin Garza

In the following viewpoint journalist Xazmin Garza dem-
onstrates that students can still find ways to express their
personalities even if they attend schools that impose dress
codes. Countering the argument that dress codes prevent
students from being seen as individuals, Garza quotes a
professional stylist who recommends ways for students to
use accessories—headbands, jewelry, shoes, and bags—
to make a statement. A principal quoted in the viewpoint argues that what is lost in terms of creativity and
self-expression is made up for by a school community's
increased focus on learning. Garza is the fashion reporter
for the *Las Vegas Review-Journal* in Clark County, Nevada,
where this viewpoint first appeared.

Seven-year-old Kayana Benson can go on and on about her
friend Avery's cool purple top that makes the shape of a
butterfly.

She got it at Target. It's "really cute." And, did she mention it
looks like a butterfly?

Kayana starts third grade soon. She can't wear anything purple. She won't get her clothes at Target. And, tops that resemble butterflies are absolutely out of the question. She attends the private Merryhill School and wears a uniform every day. While she laments the fashion freedom her neighborhood friends have at their public schools, she still finds ways to express herself, even with the strict limitations of her uniform.

The author reports that even if they all wear the same uniform, students can still find ways to express their personalities through accessorizing, such as by wearing distinctive TOMS shoes, colorful headbands, multicolored rubber bracelets, and sunglasses.

Used by permission of Jeff Parker.

"I want a lunchbox that's, like, kind of a purse," she says. "And, it, like, has designs on it, like peace signs and hearts."

When skinny jeans and puffed sleeves aren't an option, accessories become the priority. Dangly earrings, open-toed shoes, sleeveless tops and nail polish are all prohibited at Merryhill. But, Kayana can still don her favorite headbands, multicolored rubber bracelets, TOMS shoes and fake polka-dot-decorated eyeglasses.

The most recent addition to her closet came in the form of midcalf-length Converse sneakers, also known as her "Shake It Up" shoes. The moniker comes from the hit Disney show of the same name about two teenage dancers.

Her mother, Elaine Benson, says Kayana gave up the princess-themed or Hello Kitty book bags a couple of years ago.

"She thinks they're for littler kids," says Elaine. "She wants a roller backpack."

A 7-year-old girl not wanting to be confused with a kindergart-ner doesn't surprise Gail Ashburn, stylist at Fashion Show mall.

"A lot of kids don't want to feel like kids," she says.

That's why young men who wear school uniforms may be drawn to a messenger bag over a backpack. It's a style statement, but it also feels a little more "grown-up."

Ashburn recommends young girls head to the popular Justice clothing store, where trends are translated in an age-appropriate manner. Aside from headbands with big floral embellishments and sparkly bangles, she suggests uniform-wearing girls get expressive with their shoes. Studded ballet flats come to mind.

Footwear is also the best option for boys in uniform. Olympic track and field stars have popularized bright, loud sneakers. If boys want to keep it more understated, Ashburn notes that dark gray sneakers are hot for back-to-school as are canvas Vans that are "similar to boat shoes."

If dress codes are especially stringent, kids can still find creative loopholes, such as scrunching up their sleeves or popping their collars.

"If girls are feeling like they can't find their individuality," Ashburn says, "they can paint all their toes a different color. That way their secret is safe and the school will never know."

Uniforms aren't exclusively worn at private schools. Of the 325 schools in the Clark County School District, 96 participate in what's called "standard student attire."

"The idea was brought forward where it's not the principal who decides, it's the community," says Byron Green, director of instruction for the Clark County School District.

A committee of six parents, two school staff members, two students and one administrator determines the attire, and a ballot is sent to parents by mail. If 10 percent of the ballots are returned and 55 percent vote in favor of it, standard student attire is implemented. It must require the basic colors, khaki, navy and white, but additional school colors can be added.

Green says accessories generally aren't regulated. It's more about sleeve lengths, collars, where waistbands sit, etc. Sneakers, socks, belts, jewelry and hair accessories are all up to the student.

"A lot of schools like standard student attire, especially if it's a low socioeconomic school, because it's a great equalizer," Green says. "Kids may not feel bad if they don't have the most hip, stylish clothes. Everyone looks the same."

He hears from principals that it also turns the focus to achievement and learning, rather than who's cool and who's not. The downside? "It really limits creativity and self-expression," he says.

Kayana and Elaine Benson know that all too well.

Whenever her daughter expresses the desire to attend public school like some of the other kids in her neighborhood, so she can dress freely, Elaine has an answer prepared. "I just tell her she's so smart she has to go to private school," she says.

As she prepares for her back-to-school shopping this year, though, Kayana's looking at things a little differently.

"I kind of like uniforms," she says, "'cause, like, if you have clothes, you have to go, 'Um, should I wear this one or that one?'"

SIX

Dress Codes Reinforce Sexist and Homophobic Attitudes

Soraya Chemaly

In the following viewpoint Soraya Chemaly examines the assumptions that she claims often lie behind dress codes in schools—policies that emphasize the sexuality of girls and the supposed inability of boys to control themselves around girls. Dress codes that focus on traditional gender roles, she argues, are unfair to girls and to students who are not heterosexual. School policies should be based on respect for all students, rather than on harmful and unexamined stereotypes, she concludes. Chemaly writes about feminism, gender, and culture for the *Huffington Post*, the *Feminist Wire*, and other media.

Spring is coming, which means we are entering the season of the regulation of how much skin girls around the country are allowed to bare. Dress codes, while usually regulating boys' slovenliness, tend to police girls for how much of their bodies are visible. Anyone who's ever painted or stood in a room surrounded by [artist] Kara Walker silhouettes can tell you that white space is defining and when we talk about dress codes, girls' skin is the white space we've all been trained to ignore in these discussions. And, while everyone is in theory affected by dress codes, girls and LGTBQ [lesbian, gay, transgendered, bisexual, and queer or questioning] youth are disproportionately affected by them. Challenging schools to align unexamined, traditional dress codes to contemporary values is a tangible place to start if you're interested in teaching kids to live in a diverse, tolerant society. Of course, many parents are not interested.

When it comes to girls, skimpy and skin-baring clothes are often the primary issue. Kids know that many words, like "unladylike," are code for "slutty." Other words that are frequently used include "distracting" and "unprofessional." Many teachers worry that girls' skin will "so addle boys' brains that they will be unable to concentrate." Boys, and apparently in Iowa, adult men who can now legally fire "irresistible" women, we are told, simply cannot concentrate in this environment. [A 2012 Iowa Supreme Court decision affirmed the right of bosses to fire "irresistible" employees.]

So, what exactly is wrong with saying girls are "distracting"? I mean, everyone knows this, right?

Who gets to be distracted? And, whose distraction is central? What is a girl supposed to think in the morning when she wakes up and tries to decide what to wear to school? They aren't idiots. The logical conclusion of the "distracting" issue is, "Will I turn someone on if I wear this?" Now who is doing the sexualizing? My daughters would never have thought these things without the help of their school. The only people these policies worry about distracting are heterosexual boys. When I was a teenager, there was a boy who distracted the hell out of me. It was the way his hair brushed against his neck and an insouciant ease with his large body. I managed just fine academically, and so can straight boys who encounter girls they are attracted to. When have you ever heard someone talk about what is distracting to girls or gay kids? This idea ignores that fact that girls and LBGTQ kids exist as sexual people. But, do you know what is distracting? Trying not to be distracting. This framing of the problem is marginalizing, sexist and heteronormative [assuming everyone is heterosexual].

In addition, it implies strongly that girls have responsibility for boys' responses and that boys cannot control themselves. Boys

School dress codes are often based on stereotypes such as that all students are heterosexual and that girls must not look too sexy because teenage boys cannot control their sexual urges.

should be insulted. People need to get a super-firm grip on the fact that girls are not sexual thermostats for their male peers. They need to manage themselves and are fully capable of doing so.

Third, if people are concerned that girls consider themselves decorative or that they think that appearing in what can be construed as sexually provocative ways is important, then they should confront the reasons why girls perceive these things to be true by the time they are 10 or 11. The clothes that our culture makes available and fashionable for girls—the ones tied to being attractive, to glamour, success, money and public female power and glory—are the same ones that make it possible for most girls and women to access power and resources vicariously in male-dominated culture. THAT is what schools should be concerned with. Blaming girls for making rational choices about what society rewards them for is useless and hypocritical.

Comfortable and Respectful

This isn't to say girls should go to school wearing anything that strikes their fancy, no matter how skimpy. When their underwear is showing it's not because they're channelling [French fashion designer] Jean Paul Gaultier in an attempt to show how artificial the construction of gender is. There are times when girls reach an age when being sexy or sexual is just fine, but in the same way that they shouldn't wear athletic clothes to go to a wedding, they shouldn't wear clothes they'd wear, say, to a concert, when they go to school. I want my girls to be comfortable at school and respectful of their teachers and the learning environment. Boys, too. If this means, as girls occasionally suggest to teachers, that a school talk to boys about not looking at girls' legs if it makes them uncomfortable, then so be it. With uniforms, it should be even simpler. The issue isn't the rules per se, it's how they're constructed.

Equally important is how they are enforced. This is of much more concern and frequently sets harmful precedents.

Some administrators start every school day with rigorous visual inspections as kids tumble onto campuses. These inspections don't exist in a vacuum. No one is suggesting that teachers are like street harassers. But, inspections begin around the same time that young girls start experiencing daily street harassment and sexual harassment on campus. In school, boys, like girls, are targets of public humiliation but, especially if they are straight, this type of public inspection and commentary on their bodies and clothes is usually limited to school. For girls and many LGBTQ people, this is just the beginning and it never ends. They have to deal with related feelings amplified by administrators who feel strongly about enforcement. On the recent afternoon of the day that my girls' school reviewed uniform policies, a gaggle of 13-year-old girls (in regulation uniforms) piled into my car as two men on the street leered, mumbled "compliments" at them and laughed. I didn't mention it, but realized the girls heard them as they started talking about how "creepy" it was. One made an automatic and unself-conscious connection: She said she did not like being inspected in school and it felt the same way to her. It's hard to know, in this context, who a girl is talking about when she says she's "uncomfortable when he winks" at me. I know it seems ridiculous to compare thoughtful, often loving teachers—of both sexes—with random jerks on the street, but that is true only if you willfully deny the centrality of the 13-year-old girls' point of view in the matter of her own comportment. The well-documented, harmful effects of self-objectification that result from the policing of school dress regulations is not unlike those that result from street harassment. From the girls' perspective, they'd started their day with people reviewing, having conversations about and publicly commenting on their bodies and were ending it in the same manner. It's wearisome. Some might say distracting.

The Right to Bare Arms

In addition, the way school rules are often demonstrated is seriously problematic. For example, administrators might take a girl up to a stage and draw a line on her leg, to show where a regulation length skirt should fall. This is often done with humor, to offset the unpleasantness and difficulty of the task at hand, and everyone has a good laugh. A girl with no power, being told by a bigger person with authority what to do, *might be acquiescing to what is happening to her, but she is not consenting.* By using her body as a prop, the enforcer uses her body as an object for his or her purposes. Making it a joke can be insidious. I know this is not what's going through a teacher's head when surrounded by

Dress Codes and Gender Differences

In a 2001 National School Climate Survey, 14.1 percent of the lesbian, gay, bisexual, and transgender young people said they felt limited by school dress code policies that reinforce traditional gender differences.

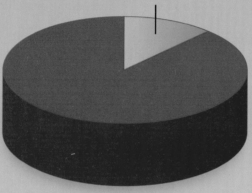

14.1%
Felt limited by school
dress code policies

Taken from: Gay, Lesbian & Straight Education Network (GLSEN). The 2011 National School Climate Survey, 2012. www.glsen.org/nscs.

pubescent students who are violating code. But, nonetheless, this happens every day, year after year in some places, and it is a terrible precedent to set for boys and girls.

Our ideas about consent and the use of other people's bodies are important and cannot, in this culture, begin early enough. Take, for example, the fact that 28% of girls in college are sexually assaulted (and 3% of boys), only 5% report these crimes. Say a boy or group of boys rapes a girl. They have grown up with ideas about how her clothes can "distract" boys and make them do things they haven't being told or asked overtly to control. The girl also might very well have internalized ideas repeatedly conveyed to her about how people confuse her clothes for "morality," or intent, how others can use or comment on her body, how her consent is not either expected or respected. Not only has she internalized these ideas, but her school might have institutionalized them in dress code policy and enforcement. This is not helpful. According to the Center for Public Integrity, only 5% of victims report crimes either because they don't understand their nature or because they are well aware of institutional tolerances for these practices.

Girls' "right to bare arms" is an idea with a long and meaningful tail.

This topic must be one of the most difficult for school administrators, often caught between a rock and a hard place with students, parents, their personal beliefs, traditions and concerns about student safety and performance. There are many ways to consider the usefulness, purpose, intent and effects of dress codes. If school communities are genuinely worried about girls and boys then they need to examine the stereotypes that permeate their own policies—policies that are sometimes simply palimpsests [coverings] of sexism, racism and homophobia, written over time and left undisturbed for too long. When traditions are sexist and homophobic they should be abandoned.

SEVEN

Dress Codes for School Dances Inappropriately Emphasize Female Students' Sexuality

Lindsay Kamikawa

In the following viewpoint Lindsay Kamikawa details what she describes as humiliating treatment that she and other young women endured at her high school's formal winter dance. Her school's policy, she argues, was vague in defining judgments such as "too tight," "too short," and "inappropriate." Dress codes for formal dances tend to emphasize female bodies, she concludes, and unfairly restrict young women's sense of comfort and style. Kamikawa, a senior at Capistrano Valley High School in California when she wrote this viewpoint, was one of the editors in chief of her school newspaper, the *Capistrano Valley High School Times*, where this viewpoint first appeared.

At Winter Formal, a Capo [Capistrano Valley High School in California] student was punched on the dance floor by one of five trespassing Yorba Linda [High School, in the town where the dance was held] students. He suffered a concussion and was later hospitalized. The administration failed to prevent the entry of the non-Capo students, but its attention was certainly prioritized elsewhere.

Clumsily and arbitrarily the administration withheld some 40 girls from the dance because their dresses violated the formal dress code, which had been set at the beginning of the school year and revised before Winter Formal. Although there were several girls who I believed had dressed inappropriately, I was among the many who felt my dress was in complete compliance with the dress code.

When Assistant Principal Leslie Schuda appropriated me to the "denied" section of the Nixon Library staircase, I considered the rules I had read on the CVHS [Capistrano Valley High School] website prior to the dance. The one which I had apparently violated was as follows: "Stretchy tight skirts/dresses are prohibited (lycra, spandex, etc.)." My dress was neither lycra nor spandex. Not only did it go past my fingertips, which was used as a determinant for appropriate length, but it also had thick, textured criss-cross ruffles throughout and didn't ride up when I walked. I saw no violation.

A sympathetic teacher brought me to Principal Kevin Astor for a reevaluation. After observing my dress from all angles, he said something to the effect of "What part of your body isn't your dress tight on?" Though I knew he was trying to be humorously disconcerting, I felt extremely uncomfortable. Later, I understood that the problem was not that my dress violated the dress code—it was that my entry to the dance was dependent on my principal's personal taste.

Subjectivity is unavoidable when it comes to judging whether a dress is appropriate. However, the loose language and poor enforcement of the Winter Formal dress code set every girl up for potential failure.

Degrading Treatment for Some?

Girls in question of violating the code were subject to degrading evaluation by staff members. Many were asked to lift their arms, walk back and forth, and stand with their backs to their administrators, two of whom were male. Dress code is supposed to ensure that students don't feel objectified. Every girl who was flagged that night had a reason to feel physically compromised.

Once moved to the staircase, we were given two options: 1) Stay outside for the remainder of the night, or 2) Have a parent drive to Yorba Linda with a more "appropriate" dress. My mother was one of the several parents that was inconvenienced by a 35 mile drive to Yorba Linda that Friday night.

As I waited for her arrival, I noticed several discrepancies in administration's judgment.

Girls exposing distracting cleavage were admitted while a girl in a conservative one-shoulder, long-sleeved flowy dress was flagged for wearing a bandeau to cover part of her side.

A girl with a curve-flaunting, mini peplum dress gained entrance while several almost identical peplum dresses were held outside.

One girl wearing a cotton-thin, body-hugging dress was approved. The fabric came well above her knees, and could have easily been categorized as a clubbing dress, which girls were told to avoid. Her only possible redemptive quality? She was thin and not curvaceous, perhaps causing the illusion of a more modest dress.

When [two] seniors asked Assistant Principal Todd Amon why some girls had been let in with the same dresses as girls who were held outside, he suggested that "different dresses fit different people." While this is true, it is unfair to employ such an explanation for violating dress code because it leads girls to the question, "Is my body the problem?" For senior [A.T.], it was.

Though [A.T.] had already been cleared by an administrator ten minutes prior, she was summoned back to the dance entrance, where Dr. Astor deemed her dress "too short." Unlike the girls who were wearing nearly identical dresses inside, [A.T.] is 6'2".

"I was never ashamed of my body until that night," she said. "I was humiliated."

Shifting Standards

Administration finally reevaluated the dresses of the girls outside, letting many in. I was speechless. Apparently the dress code standards had changed within an hour period. Why couldn't these have been implemented from the beginning?

Would You Support a Dress Code for the High School Prom?

In an unscientific poll, Nickelodeon Parent Connect asked visitors to its website to weigh in on the subject of dress codes for school proms.

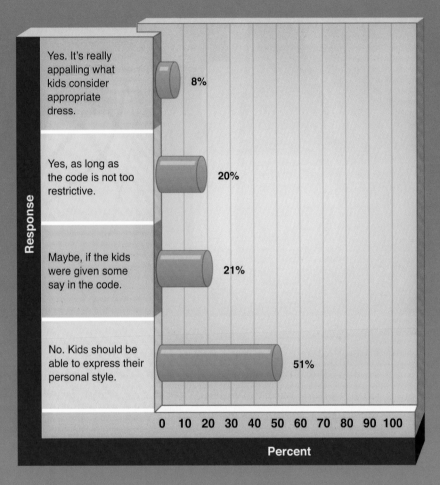

Taken from: Nickelodeon Parents Connect, 2013. www.parentsconnect.com/parenting–your–kids/parenting–teenagers /learning–and–school/support_prom_dresscode.html.

At around 9:30 PM, two-and a-half hours into the dance, there was a second reevaluation. Girls who were flagged for wearing dresses with cutouts or bandeaus were let in. But the girls wearing "tight" dresses were given the option to either stay outside or

These young ladies' prom dresses were deemed "inappropriate" for their school prom. Prom dress codes vary from school to school regarding what is considered proper, which often leads to students' confusion about just what constitutes inappropriate dress.

complete a 4 hour Saturday school, in addition to having their dresses approved by administration before Prom, should they decide to go. Not surprisingly, all 13 of the girls opted for the latter. Still, girls wearing tight dresses hadn't violated the dress code any more than every other girl who had been flagged—there was no reason for them to receive a more severe punishment.

Senior [L.B.] was among the thirteen that reluctantly signed her name to the Saturday school list. Although she was confident her dress would not receive dress code [violations], as it went past her fingertips and had a conservative cut, it was still considered too tight by administration.

"If I had thought my dress to be inappropriate, by the school's standards as well as by my own, I would not have worn it. When I put on that dress, I thought it was classy; I still have no idea why I was given dress code," [she] said.

What Is Too Tight?

Dress code needs to have rules that can be enforced practically. The use of subjective qualifiers such as "too tight" makes it difficult for girls to understand why their dresses were inappropriate, and thereby correct their mistakes for the future. It is unfair, and a true testament to the level of subjectivity, that several girls were let in by the female administrators, Ms. Schuda and Assistant Principal Jaime Carman, but were then recalled by Dr. Astor. Unless the rules are concise, administration is free to disapprove of dresses without a reason that could be proven to students, defeating the purpose of dress code entirely.

Dress code raises many complex issues. At Winter Formal, why was only female dress code taken to such ridiculous extremes? Whose responsibility is it to judge whether a dress on a girl makes sense? It is easy to tell boys that they cannot wear hats at school or Dickies [casual pants] to formal dances. But to tell a teenage girl that she cannot wear a dress because it is "too tight" begs the question: What is too tight?

Just because I wear a dress that fits my figure does not mean that I want to sexualize my body, which is implied in being told by my principal that my dress is "too tight." It is not the administration's responsibility to determine whether my body in a certain dress is inappropriately alluring to other students, especially when they take evaluations to such bizarre extremes.

Capo is the only high school in the Capistrano Unified and Saddleback Valley Unified that has strict prohibitions on strapless dresses, dress cutouts and dress tightness. In the future, our school should consider the community standards and pursue a code that is more similar to those of neighboring schools.

"For Prom, I am hopeful that we will have a meeting with students, administration and staff members so that there's participation by all stakeholders," Schuda said.

"Any other clothing deemed inappropriate by the CVHS administration"—the final dress code prohibition on our dance contracts. This is the area of concern; the shadow between objective and subjective, entrance and inconvenience, a concussion and a safe night of fun. If administration focuses more on what really matters, that is, making sure students feel comfortable at dances, then perhaps it won't have to rely so heavily on this fallible and inconsistent rule.

EIGHT

The Constitution Allows Schools to Impose Dress Codes, Within Limits

Roberta F. Green and Heather B. Osborn

In the following viewpoint attorneys Roberta F. Green and Heather B. Osborn outline the legal considerations that should be balanced when a school creates a dress code. A student's right to free expression is guaranteed under the First Amendment to the US Constitution, the authors point out, but that right is not unlimited, and a school may restrict students' rights to wear clothing with messages that undermine a positive school environment. The courts have tended to support administrators' rights to limit sexual remarks on shirts, the authors state, but have generally opposed dress codes that regulate political speech. Green and Osborn practice law with the firm of Shuman McCuskey & Slicer, in West Virginia.

A public school student's right of free speech can frequently come into conflict with school officials' authority to prescribe and control conduct. This nexus is probably nowhere more evident than in dress codes and school uniforms. While school uniforms seem like a safe and easy choice, litigation abounds related to how the decision is made to wear uniforms, whether it is permissible to have the school logo and slogan on the uniform, and whether alternative, adequate outlets for speech exist.

Roberta F. Green and Heather B. Osborn, "Legal Matters: Successful Dress Codes," *Communicator*, vol. 36, no. 9, May 2013. Reprinted with permission. Copyright © 2013. National Association of Elementary School Principals. All rights reserved.

The U.S. Supreme Court has provided broad guidance as to what regulation of speech by educators is permissible, but, notably, the tests are largely fact-driven. In other words, nothing is very simple.

The Issues

A few precepts do arise—the rules to take home, if you will—that can guide decision-makers early in this process. While students have First Amendment rights that are not as broad as those of adults in a public forum, they do have those rights, nonetheless. Any limitation upon those rights must be measured in light of the special characteristics of the school environment. Schools may regulate speech consistently with legitimate pedagogical concerns, which include increasing student achievement, promoting safety, teaching manners and habits conducive to happiness and self-government, and enhancing a positive school environment. And the Court has recognized that these goals may necessitate some limitations on speech. However, those limitations must be merely a byproduct of the pedagogical concern—not the goal.

The constitutional issue with dress codes and/or uniforms is that dress constitutes free expression, which in the legal analysis is speech. The initial question is whether the prohibition of speech/dress is based on the content of the speech or the manner in which the speech is expressed.

The Cases

Specifically, one of the early watershed cases on school dress—*Tinker v. Des Moines Independent Community School District* [1969]—considered whether students could be stopped from wearing black armbands to school in protest of the Vietnam War. Upon learning of the students' protest plans, the school intervened and, prior to the protest, the school adopted a policy that any student wearing a black armband to school would be suspended until s/he returned without the armband.

While the era of black armbands may have largely passed, the *Tinker* case has come to stand for the proposition that a school's fear or apprehension of a disturbance is not enough to overcome the students' rights of free expression. As a practical matter, *Tinker* has allowed a student to wear an offensive or controversial T-shirt unless or until an actual disturbance breaks out. For example, a parent made a T-shirt for her fifth grade son; the shirt included a slogan on the back that read, "Even Adults Lie." The reference arose from an altercation at the school in which the fifth grader purportedly was unfairly maligned by a teacher; the shirt appeared the next day. The reviewing court found that the fifth grader could wear the shirt and could even explain the circumstances of the shirt. However, when the fifth grader became belligerent about the shirt, yelling and disrupting hallways until fisticuffs ensued,

The constitutional issue that arises around school dress codes is that dress constitutes free expression, which is considered a form of free speech, a First Amendment right.

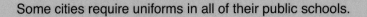

Citywide Uniform Policies

Some cities require uniforms in all of their public schools.

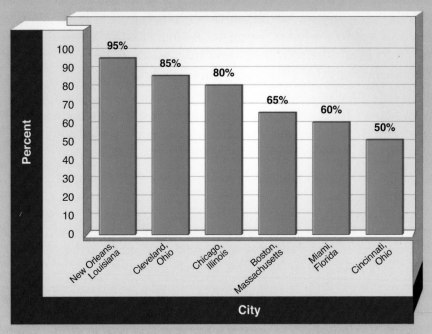

Taken from: Education Bug, 2013. www.educationbug.org/a/public-school-uniform-statistics.html.

then the shirt/speech had created a disturbance and the school could intervene.

So, the initial determinant is whether the speech or clothing is actually disruptive, not whether it is expected to be disruptive. Therefore, administrators who have stopped students at the door and waylaid them until the attire was changed have been found to have acted precipitously. That said, courts have found as well that some speech is, on its face, not conducive to civil discourse and is inappropriate for school generally, including inflammatory religious messages (e.g., "Islam is of the Devil" in *Sapp v. School Board of Alachua County, Florida*, 2011). That is true as well of speech that is lewd, vulgar, and inappropriate for the maturity level of the audiences—then, the school may intervene. For example, in

Bethel School Dist. v. Fraser (1986), the Court found in favor of the school when considering a student's use of sexually suggestive speech at a school-sponsored assembly for student body elections.

Dress codes raise additional issues, both in terms of their adoption (which needs to allow parents their due process rights) and the nature of the code itself. For example, a code would need to further an important or substantial government interest that is unrelated to suppression of free speech, such as increased safety or improved academic performance. The restriction must go no further than essential to advance that interest.

One factor that courts have considered is the countervailing effort the schools have given to ensuring "speech" in other forms—allowing students to select their own footwear or jewelry, allowing students a "free speech" alley for voicing their issues, allowing non-uniform days periodically to allow for speech or even identifying one school in the district as a "non-uniform school" for persons who wish to opt out.

The Recommendations

In summary, a school considering limiting speech will want to consider whether it is the content or the manner of speech being regulated. If it is the content, the test may include whether disruption occurred or was only expected or forecasted to occur. If it is the manner of speech, then the propriety of that speech for the audience is a determinant (and most of these cases deal with sexually charged situations, as opposed to political speech or violence). Thus, perhaps the truest statement that can be made about speech and dress codes is that the determinations are based on facts and on the motivation of the school administrators.

NINE

Dress Codes Help Prepare Students for Life After School

Terri Bryce Reeves

> In the following viewpoint Terri Bryce Reeves describes the first day of school at a Florida high school that had imposed a new dress code over the summer—a parent-supported code that she calls one of the strictest in the state. The principal explains that the dress code is part of a new effort at the school to prepare students for their futures as professionals; dressing for success will help them be successful, he believes. The viewpoint concludes with quotes from a mother and several students, who generally accept that the new dress code will be positive for them and for their school. Reeves is a correspondent for the *Tampa Bay Times*, where this viewpoint first appeared.

About two dozen students didn't follow Clearwater High School's [in Florida] new modified dress code on Monday [August 20, 2012].

But about 2,000 others did, making the first day of the school year for the Tornadoes [the school mascot and nickname] a roaring success.

"It's been a great day," said principal Keith Mastorides. "The tone on campus this morning was very positive and calm—and we're hoping that will continue."

Last spring, parents voted in favor of what is considered the strictest dress code for a public high school in Pinellas County [Florida].

Under the new rules, students can wear polo and dress shirts and blouses in solid colors of red, white, gray or black, to reflect the school's colors. Official Clearwater High T-shirts are also permitted.

Pants, shorts and skirts may be black, khaki or gray, and must be worn up to the waist and down to the knee. Jeans are fine as long as they are neat and not torn.

The current trend in school dress codes is that students may wear polo and dress shirts and blouses in solid colors or T-shirts in the school's colors with the school's name.

Gone are hoodies, nonschool T-shirts, bare midriffs, torn pants, shorts and skirts above the knee, bedroom slippers and pajamas, which were often accompanied with a blanket for that "just rolled out of bed look." Cleavage and underwear cannot be visible.

Dressing for Success

Mastorides said the dress code goes hand in hand with the school's new "wall to wall" academy model that will help prepare students for the professional world by offering industry certification in four areas: business and international studies; technology, math and engineering; arts and media; and sports and recreation.

"It's all about teaching the kids to dress for success—teaching them to dress for the real world," he said.

On Monday, no one was sent home for a dress code violation, according to Mastorides. Rather, they were handed Clearwater High T-shirts or their parents were called to bring in clothes. The school's PTA [parent-teacher association] and the Clothes To Kids organization are standing by to help those in need meet the new requirements.

Laquinta Hardy, 15, said some of her friends were mad about the new rules at first, but they've since come around. She couldn't wait for the first day of school "to see how people are wearing their new 'uniforms,'" she said.

The school day started with an MTV-like video created by students.

It features students dressed in red, white, gray or black driving convertibles of the same colors. A rap promotes the benefits of the new code.

Reed Avers, 17, used to wear basketball shorts to school. On this day, though, he was wearing khaki shorts—with the required belt.

"They're comfortable but not as comfortable as the gym shorts," he said. "It's really not that bad of a dress code. It shows that the staff cares about us and wants us to be successful."

Although not required, many of the staff and teachers also followed suit.

Dressing for Success

In a 2008 survey by CareerBuilder.com, 41 percent of employers said that they are more likely to promote employees who dress professionally.

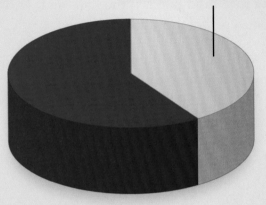

41%
Employers more likely to promote those who dress professionally

Taken from: Careerbuilder.com. "Forty-One Percent of US Employers More Likely to Promote Employees Who Wear Professional Attire, Reveals CareerBuilder.com Survey," June 17, 2008. www.careerbuilder.com/share/aboutus/press releasesdetail.aspx?id=pr438&sd=6%2F17%2F2008&ed=12%2F31%2F2008.

Nicole Allen, 17, likes the stricter rules. No longer is she faced with agonizing decisions about what to wear.

"It cuts a lot of time in the morning so I can sleep longer," she said.

Others wished there were more color and pattern options—and they'll miss their hoodies—but in general, they seemed satisfied.

Margaret Bello, 17, took advantage of the fact that there are no rules against belts, scarves, jewelry and other accessories. She wore an orange tie belt wrapped around her white blouse for "a little splash of color."

James Tanton, 17, a football player, predicted the code will promote school pride and make the school less divisive.

"It's a uniform dress code for a uniform student body," he said.

Mom Missy Russell said she has supported the new dress code from the beginning.

"As a parent it makes getting up in the morning much easier. We save time and get to sleep in a little longer. There's no arguing. Less frustration. It's easier on the shopping and much better on the budget."

She sensed a positive buzz in the hallways on Monday morning.

"It's nice to walk down the halls and see everyone look like they are a part of the school," she said.

TEN

Litchfield Elementary School District's Teacher Dress Code Sparking Questions

Eddi Trevizo

In the following viewpoint Eddi Trevizo highlights a relatively new trend in public schools: dress codes for teachers and principals. Like many students who deal with clothing restrictions, many teachers argue that the language of their own dress codes is too vague and that enforcement is not always fair, while administrators argue that teachers need to dress professionally to set an example for students. Flexibility is important when drafting a dress code, the viewpoint concludes. Trevizo is a reporter who covers education for the *Arizona Republic*.

Blue hair, "extreme" hairstyles, facial piercings, distracting tattoos and "excessive" earrings are all prohibited under a new dress code in the Litchfield Elementary School District [in Arizona].

The rules aren't for students. The policy is for teachers and principals, but is especially aimed at the district's more than 600 teachers. The code was written to promote modesty and professionalism, district officials said. The board approved the policy July 10 [2012].

Some education officials familiar with the issue say the new dress code may be one of the most restrictive among metro Phoenix public schools. Many of the area's largest school districts ask teachers to dress professionally and to cover offensive tattoos. But in some smaller school districts, boards have tougher dress codes for teachers.

At a time when tattoos, edgy hair colors and facial piercings have lost their shock value, some teachers worry that dress codes are open to broad interpretation and are concerned about how the rules will be enforced.

The Litchfield rules show how one school district has grappled with balancing employees' personal freedom with a professional work environment.

Meanwhile, employment experts caution that dress codes must take into account legal issues, including employees from different cultural and religious backgrounds.

The Litchfield district is headquartered in Litchfield Park, but includes 13 schools and more than 10,000 students in elementary and middle schools in Goodyear, Avondale, Buckeye and Litchfield Park.

For district teachers, the dress code creates many questions, said Carol Klein, a first-grade teacher in the district.

"Where do they draw the line?" Klein asked. "I know a teacher with a tattoo on her wrist that says 'faith.' Is that appropriate or inappropriate?"

She agrees with most of the new regulations, but thinks the board needs to define terms such as "excessive," "extreme" and "distracting" so that teachers are better informed.

Looking Professional

Like many employers, the district is trying to maintain a professional work atmosphere in changing times.

District leaders created the policy because the organization didn't have a written policy and thought it was time to create one, said Shawn Watt, governing board president.

Vague Teacher Dress Codes

A 2008 study of teachers' employee manuals found that most required teachers to dress "professionally" or "appropriately." Many of these manuals failed to provide specific examples of professional or appropriate dress.

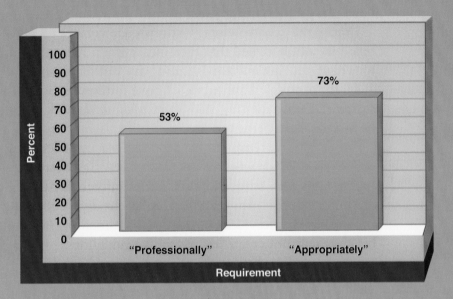

Taken from: Beth W. Freeburg and Jane E. Workman. "Results from Illinois University Council for Career and Technical Education 2007–2008 Awards for Innovation Project," 2008; Jane E. Workman, and Beth W. Freeburg. "A Clear Definition of Appropriate Dress for Teachers." Illinois University Council for Career and Technical Education Awards for Innovation Proposal. www.iluccte.org/Workman_and_Freeburg_AFI.pdf.

There have not been a lot of complaints about teachers who are dressed unprofessionally, district officials said.

Sara Griffin, a Litchfield governing board member, drafted most of the regulations for hair color, piercings, tattoos and clothing in the new policy. Griffin said tattoos, especially tattoos that cover the entire arm, can appear unprofessional, offensive or distracting.

"It should not be modeled as a norm from such a young age," Griffin has said at previous meetings.

The rules include prohibitions common in many workplaces. That includes rubber flip-flops, visible undergarments, visible cleavage and bare midriffs.

Employees also can't wear clothes that are too tight, loose or transparent, short skirts or exercise pants. Tops may not bare shoulders.

Men would be required to wear shirts with a collar except under conditions such as school spirit days.

But other rules, which limit hairstyles, piercings and tattoos, have generated more debate.

During the debate before the dress-code vote, Watt and other board members argued that piercings, certain hairstyles and tattoos have become mainstream and have lost major shock value.

"A lot of people have tattoos. I have tattoos. It shouldn't be a matter of personal taste," said Watt, adding, "I think we need to be careful about being too specific."

An earlier, more restrictive proposal was considered but not adopted because of concerns from Watt and other board members.

Principals and school administrators enforce day-to-day rules on staff conduct and appearance. Under the dress code, administrators may develop more restrictive guidelines for their campus, but they may not create less restrictive guidelines.

Other smaller districts have implemented similar rules, but don't include things like hair color.

Gilbert Public Schools and the Peoria Unified School District have dress codes similar to Litchfield's that regulate skirt length, appropriate shoes and apparel, facial piercings, offensive tattoos, and accessories.

Strict dress codes have several benefits, supporters say.

Written standards empower principals and administrators in charge of staff dress codes. Many policies are also written to keep staff safe in emergencies, or when operating heavy equipment in classes. Dress codes also help teachers to be better role models to students, supporters said.

Rae Conelley, principal at Frontier Elementary School in the Peoria district, said the new policy addressed modesty concerns at her school.

"There were some teachers that were relieved (when the policy was adopted). They had felt uncomfortable about some of the choices that colleagues would wear in terms of modesty," Conelley said.

Dress codes for teachers are a relatively new trend in public schools and are viewed as a means to promote the values of modesty and professionalism among teachers.

Larger School Districts

Larger school districts have grappled with similar issues but adopted a more flexible policy.

Mesa Public Schools, the largest district in Arizona with 82 schools and more than 63,000 students, doesn't have a written dress code other than general conduct guidelines promoting professionalism, said Helen Hollands, director of communications.

Visible tattoos and accessories cannot convey messages related to illegal substances, tobacco, alcohol, violence, gangs, or obscene language or images. Principals address the topic of professional dress throughout the school year.

Other districts follow similar standards. The Phoenix Union High School District and Dysart Unified School District don't have written regulations that list prohibited apparel, accessories, piercings or tattoos.

"We want to treat teachers like professionals and not like children. Sometimes those types of rules are not good for morale," said Craig Pletenik, community relations manager for Phoenix Union.

Legal Issues

At a time when education leaders are coping with salary, budget, student-performance and accountability issues, dress codes have not been a major issue, said Ed Bufford, a teacher in Phoenix Union and member of the Phoenix Union Classroom Teachers Association.

"What it boils down to is that one person's opinion is different than another's. We encourage people to dress professionally for their position in a manner that doesn't create an issue," Bufford said.

As schools try to strike a balance [between] professional dress and changing social norms, employers need to build in some flexibility when they craft a dress code, said John Balitis, an attorney at Phoenix-based law firm Fennemore Craig.

Balitis said fair policies don't necessarily have to provide specific examples of distracting, inappropriate or offensive grooming.

He recommends setting a basic standard of practice that still allows wiggle room for religious beliefs or groups that could be affected retroactively by new policies.

Religious ornaments, garments, piercings or tattoos are subject to protection even if some people find them to be excessive or distracting. The litmus test is to verify the attire or grooming is a fundamental practice within that religion.

"People of certain faiths have to display certain things or dress a certain way as a sincere part of their religious beliefs," Balitis said.

Still, issues can arise when subjective policies are enforced by more than one person. Litchfield's new dress code must be enforced by school principals.

"A subjective policy always sets up the possibility that two people could get treated differently for wearing the same thing, depending on who is making the call," Balitis said.

ELEVEN

Students and Teachers Should Wear Academic Robes

Audrey Price

In the following viewpoint Audrey Price recommends requiring all students and teachers to wear academic robes, as university students and professors did generations ago and as characters in the Harry Potter novels did at Hogwarts School of Witchcraft and Wizardry. Although the idea seems funny, she argues that it would achieve a serious purpose: preventing the waste of time and energy that occurs when teachers and students struggle with dress codes. Requiring robes would simplify life for teachers, parents, administrators, and students, she concludes. Price teaches seventh- and eighth-grade language arts in South Carolina and writes a blog titled *True Talks on Information & Myths in Education.*

JK Rowling got it right—robes.
    Laugh first, swear you wouldn't do it or make your child do it, then consider the logical results. *Bear in mind, I think teachers should follow the same dress code as students.*

Simplification

1) I suggest a solid color robe, either in standard collegiate black or in the more typical high-school fashion of school colors. Except for white. For obvious reasons it would be ridiculous to put students in white robes. They can be purchased in heavy or light-weight fabrics for seasonal differences. It needs to be thick enough that whatever the student wears underneath will not show through. School has 2 colors? Girls can wear one, the boys the alternate, or *teachers* can wear one color while students wear the alternate. For identification purposes, teacher could also simply wear black.

2) The robe needs to zip *from the bottom to the top*, with the opening of the zipper large enough to slip over a half-inch button at the top of the zipper teeth where the collar opens. The button will then fasten closed through a button-hole supporting the zipper between the 2 layers of fabric and preventing it from accidentally coming open during the academic day.

3) Length made easy. The fact that these robes could potentially last more than one year means they need to be long enough to accommodate student growth. Robes should be past the knees *at least as long as* the student's hand is wide. . . .

What to Wear Underneath It: Keep It Simple

1) Shoes: Hard-soled, closed-toe, closed-heel shoes. I don't want to fight the laced/unlaced, fastened/unfastened frustration. Is it a flip-flop or is it a sandal? Are those socks or are they shoes or are they bedroom slippers? Shoes need to provide covering over the feet for *safety*. Period. If the back-of-the-ankle support moves or can be removed (like in Crocs or high heel dress shoes) they do not meet the dress code. If the shoe can easily be folded in half, like a bedroom slipper, they do not meet the dress code.

2) Socks: If socks are visible, they must match the color of the robe.

3) Jewelry: In light of the "I ♥ Boobies" [breast cancer aware-ness campaign] complications, visible jewelry is limited to a watch with no writing on the band. Upperclassmen and teachers may wear a class ring. Engaged/married teachers may wear an engagement ring and/or wedding ring. Engaged/married students (in case the situation occurs) may wear an engagement ring with parent endorsement or a wedding ring provided they show a marriage license.

4) Clothing that shows through at the collar or at the legs. The collar can be hidden with the cover-ups that come with robes, if the school wants to address that issue or simply mandate that it be a solid color or that no writing is visible. At the leg, keep it limited to a solid color. Anything that is visible outside of the robe must be a solid color with no writing. That's easy to enforce, easy to address, and easy to rectify.

Some people believe that requiring both students and teachers to wear academic robes (shown) is a good policy.

Realistically, a student can comfortably wear a sweater and jeans with boots or a t-shirt and shorts with tennis shoes under the robe. The child could feasibly wear the same clothes every day and no one would know it.

Out of Compliance

1) Students who are out of dress code simply go to the restroom and remove the out-of-code article of clothing. The robe is thick enough to accommodate wearing it with nothing underneath. The offensive article is placed in the office and returned to a parent whenever the parent is able to come pick it up. If the student is uncomfortable with wearing nothing under the robe, they can always put on their PE uniform or call a parent to bring something else. Very little class time need be lost addressing this circumstance.

2) Shoes are the only factor complicating this process, and I personally think it ought to be a fine on the parent the second and subsequent times a child is out of dress code for shoes. The parent and/or student can either pay the fine or complete community service at the school to pay for the fine at the going minimum wage rate of pay for work.

Logical Results

1) As a teacher I no longer have to check for nor address:
   - inappropriate, offensive, or suggestive language on clothing
   - shirt untucked
   - pants sagging too low
   - shirts too big/long
   - belt loops
   - belts
   - multi-color socks
   - undershirt matching dress code
   - logo/brand name on shirt too large or is visible
   - hoodies
   - shirts too short, showing bare skin

- shirt-sleeve vs. cap-sleeve vs. tank top
- bra straps showing
- underwear showing
- holes in clothing
- patches under holes in clothing
- shirt collars too low, showing too much cleavage
- pants gaping open in back, showing bare buttocks
- one pant leg up, one pant leg down
- sweat pants or athletic pants
- drawstring or elastic waistband
- are those leggings or really tight pants

2) As a parent I no longer need to buy a set of school uniforms and a set of at home/play clothes. Robes cost from $15 each for the light-weight material to $90 for the heavier, more winter-weather appropriate materials. Prices generally average $25 . . . per well-made multi-use gown. If the school orders them in bulk, they can be discounted even further. It would be economical to purchase 2 of each type of robe with the plans for the student to wear them for 2 years. At an expense of $100 for 2 *years* of school clothes, I have saved money and even if the school ends up having to provide the robes, it would be feasible to reuse robes from year to year and to loan them out rather than give them away.

3) As a school administrator I could color co-ordinate the robes per grade level and quickly identify a student who might be in an out-of-area situation. Or, I could have all the students wear the same color and make it less obvious which students are 6th graders and which are 8th graders, which are freshmen and which are seniors so that less negative peer interaction occurred. Honors students or students with perfect attendance might be rewarded with bars on sleeves.

4) As a student
   - I can wear my PE uniform under my robe, and I never have to be embarrassed about dressing out in front of my peers again. I take off my robe for PE and put it back on after PE, probably with a lot of deodorant added. Or more realistically, I wear my PE uniform under my robe,

bring a clean change of clothes for after PE and I only have to change one time at school.

- If I play sports I can wear my practice clothes or game uniform under my robe.
- If I'm older and have an after-school job, I can wear my work uniform under my robe and make it faster to get to work when I finish classes for the day.
- If I'm a girl and I have an "accident" at school, no one will see it because my robe will cover up my pants.

Finally, if I want to bring the whole ensemble together with a student ID, the badge can easily be clipped onto the button-hole

Class Time Lost to Dress Code Enforcement

Barbara Bush Middle School Referrals as of November 1, 2005
386 Total

In a 2005 study of the first eight weeks of the academic year at Barbara Bush Middle School in Irving, Texas, researchers found that 40 percent of discipline referrals were related to students not following the school's dress code.

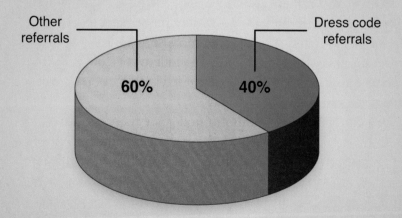

Other referrals — 60%

Dress code referrals — 40%

Taken from: Kevin Lacefield. "Dress Code Discipline Referrals: Barbara Bush Middle School," 2005.
http://cfbstaff.ctbisd.edu/lacefieldk/Dress%20Code%20Project.htm.

at the top of the zipper/collar and the student is clearly identified by the colored robe and identification at his or her neck.

The idea of wearing a robe as the students do in JK Rowling's novels seems laughable, but when given the amount of time dedicated to establishing a complicated dress code along with time spent enforcing a complicated dress code, it is undeniable the robes eliminate 90% of the problems and work load. Even parents are released from the burden of buying name brand clothing since it won't be visible anyway. This is something public school uniforms attempt yet fail to do since wealthier students purchase uniforms from Lands End or Gap or Old Navy while poorer students receive Walmart and Kmart gift cards from the schools in order to buy $100 worth of uniforms.

As a teacher, I want to do whatever it takes to make the enforcing of rules less of a burden. My focus should be teaching, not checking for holes in the wrong places or measuring large logos on shirts. And ultimately I don't want to be held responsible for determining whether or not "boobies" infringes on anyone's freedom of speech or points me out as not supporting the fight against breast cancer.

TWELVE

Many Students Accept the Necessity of Dress Codes

Hannah Gordon

In the following viewpoint Hannah Gordon explores student attitudes toward high school dress codes and concludes that many students view them positively. Some agree that a few students dress too provocatively for school but think that most high schoolers are mature enough to make good decisions about what they wear. Others point to what they see as an unfair advantage that young women have in being allowed to carry large purses throughout the day. But Gordon concludes that most students, though they may have suggestions for refinements, see the dress codes as beneficial. When she wrote this viewpoint, Gordon was a high school senior at Immaculata Academy in Buffalo, New York, and a writer for the award-winning youth section of the *Buffalo News*.

Schools have always had dress codes. Some rules were made for safety precautions, others simply to regulate indecent attire. But are public schools taking it too far? Area students have conflicting opinions. Brittany Packard, a senior at Lackawanna High School [in Buffalo, New York], says that there is nothing wrong with her school's regulations on attire.

"I think our current dress code is fine; it gets the job done without being really strict," Brittany said. Mike Lepkowski, a senior at Orchard Park High School, has a similar opinion.

"I think dress codes are good and needed, but flawed in a few places," Mike said.

However, students from Frontier and West Seneca West high schools [in Buffalo] see things very differently. "I think it's a major subtract from freedom of speech but a necessary point of contention," says Trek Fulater, a senior from West Seneca West. "While I believe fully [in] the ability to remove profanity and sexually charged comments, some of the things like cheer clothing and chains are just forms of self-expression."

Trek also mentioned that enforcing the dress code is an obstacle that gets in the way of class time. "I think that the rules forcing teachers to go after violators interrupts the learning process and is ultimately a doomed endeavor. It doesn't change anything," he said.

Jillian Pappagallo, a senior at West Seneca West, has a different bone to pick with the school's dress code.

"It doesn't handle the girls who wear short shorts and pencil skirts with revealing shirts," Jillian says. "I would love to make a specific rule that stated that girls can't wear the least amount of clothing possible." Courtney Browning, a senior at Frontier, disagrees, saying that it's the students' responsibility and dress codes aren't necessary.

"I think that schools definitely go overboard on the dress codes," Courtney said. "Some of them I understand are put in effect because they think students' clothes are too revealing or distracting to other students. But in all other cases I don't think they are needed. By high school you should be mature enough to handle the way people dress and mature enough to know what is school-appropriate and what isn't."

However, Frontier Principal Jeffrey Sortisio believes that Frontier's dress code is necessary. "We are very clear that we are not the fashion police," Sortisio said. "Our goal is not to judge students' attire in terms of aesthetic acceptability. As a large suburban high school, we have all genre of students represented.

They are free to express themselves within reason and within the tenets of the code of conduct. Dress that is deemed distracting to the school environment is prohibited. Basically, one student's idea of fashion cannot interfere with another's opportunity to learn. As with all areas of the code of conduct, we strive to be fair and consistent. I do think we meet that mark more often than not." But what about those students who don't care what is school-appropriate and what isn't? Perhaps if dress codes were more lenient, the only students affected would be the ones truly dressing indecently. "As long as nothing is showing completely or see-through then I think it's fine," Courtney said. "As hot as the school gets, if I wore shorts down to my fingertips, I would be sweating all day."

Brittany mentioned the heat as well. "The only thing I'd change is for it to allow us to wear modest tank tops (two-finger width straps) because it gets pretty warm toward the end of the year."

Bag It

Aside from the obvious articles of clothing addressed in a dress code handbook, West Seneca West also has regulations on students carrying bags. Female students are allowed to carry any sort of bags they choose, despite the unenforced rule that states bags must be folder-sized or smaller, and male students are prohibited from carrying anything.

"It's ridiculous," Trek said. "I think it's absolutely horrific that the West Seneca administration bent over for all of the girls and then enforced the bag policy on the guys. Enough with the double rule." Jillian agrees. "I don't think its fair that the girls are allowed to carry around the oversized bags and the guys can't carry the drawstring bags."

She believes it would be better (and much more fair) to allow everyone to carry bags and just regulate the size.

"Girls don't need the bags as big as a suitcase inside school," she said. "They only serve as a cover-up for texting. As for their feminine products, there are other means to hide them or keep them safe." While West Seneca West's dress code doesn't specifi-

Many students view dress codes as necessary and positive.

cally state anything regarding bags, Principal Jay Brinker, who has been principal for a year, is investigating the source of the rule.

"I never knew where the bag issue came from," Brinker said. "At the end of last year when students came to me and said, 'Mr. Brinker, the boys can never wear bags,' I saw a bit of inequality. I started my safety team on why do we have this rule, why do we have this and what are the recommendations from the FBI or the

In a 2009 survey of working adults in Japan, a country where most students are required to wear uniforms, 60 percent said that they liked wearing uniforms when they were in school.

Question: Did you like the uniforms when you where in school?

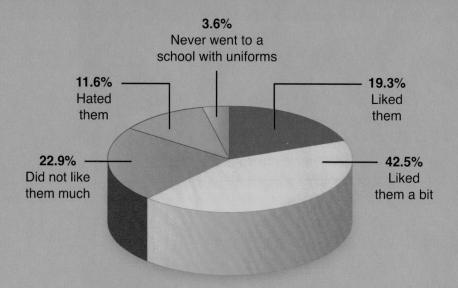

3.6%
Never went to a
school with uniforms

11.6%
Hated
them

19.3%
Liked
them

22.9%
Did not like
them much

42.5%
Liked
them a bit

Taken from: Type Research Online. "School Uniforms Kept in One in Four Japanese Women's Closets." WhatJapanThinks.com, June 2, 2009. http://whatjapanthinks.com/2009/06/05/school-uniforms-kept-in-one-in -four-japanese-womens–closets/. Original source (in Japanese): http://release.center.jp/2009/06/0202.html.

secret service on carrying bags. What are parents', students' and faculty opinions on this issue?"

The Importance of Student Input

Brinker is determined on finding the reasons behind the rule as well as setting equal standards for both male and female students. He even took a leap of faith and put school funding into buying mesh drawstring bags for the students, especially the boys, to use.

"I didn't think the students would go for it. I thought maybe we'd sell the hundred we ordered over the summer over the course of a few school years, maybe even just this one if we were lucky," he said. "We sell them in the school store for $5 and . . . about 250 have sold already. We'll sell them at cost for $7.50 [in] October [2012]."

Despite the general acceptance of the mesh bags in the student population, Brinker still wants to get to the bottom of the issue and have the ability to explain why the rule is in place when students ask. "I like my job. I like working with kids, I really do," Brinker said. "I want them to come and talk to me, most of the time they want to talk about rules. I have three daughters. I like to explain why. I don't just say, 'Don't touch the hot stove,' let me tell you why you shouldn't, why it's not allowed. Right now I don't have those answers but I can assure you I will."

The general consensus seems to be that school dress codes are necessary, but in some cases too strict in certain areas and not strict enough on the rules that really need to be enforced.

Brittany offered one last thought on the matter: "I think dress codes are needed. They are there to make the school look presentable. Well-dressed students make the school look more put together."

THIRTEEN

Dress Codes Should Be Written with Input from Students

Brenda J. Buote

In the following viewpoint Brenda J. Buote describes a controversy over a new dress code adopted in a New Hampshire high school in 2012. The controversy centers on the code's prohibition of students wearing sleeveless and cap-sleeve shirts that expose their arms and on the actions of one student, Elizabeth Skerry, who attracted national attention by publicly challenging the code. The code should be reviewed, the district superintendent concluded, and the views of students should be included in the discussion. Buote is a correspondent for the *Boston Globe*, where this viewpoint was first published.

As the sun slips behind the clouds, a cool breeze makes the leaves dance and chills the air. But Elizabeth Skerry, engrossed in a subject that has preoccupied her for the past month, seems not to notice the fading light and plummeting temperatures.

Dressed in a cap-sleeve blouse and black knee-skimming skirt, she is talking about the new student dress code at her high school. The policy, drafted by faculty over the summer [of 2012], expressly prohibits sleeveless shirts.

Bare shoulders, the administrators posit, are a distraction at the 1,413-student Timberlane Regional High School in Plaistow, N.H.

"I don't see how shoulders are a distraction," said Skerry, who was branded a scofflaw by high school principal Donald H. Woodworth for wearing her cap-sleeve blouse to class the first day of school. "But that's what the administrators keep saying, 'Bare arms are a distraction in class.'"

Upset and embarrassed, Skerry, a straight-A student who speaks with a maturity that belies her 17 years, took her case to the School Board on Sept. 20 [2012] and has launched an online campaign to amend the dress code. Her Facebook page, wittily dubbed "The Right to BARE Arms," promotes a petition that asks school officials to allow students to don sensible sleeveless dresses and tops. Nearly 300 students have signed it.

"In a school with limited air conditioning, for optimum learning to take place, the students need to be comfortable," the petition states. It urges the administration to "take all necessary action to reinstate sleeveless tops and dresses" into the dress code, including "all sleeveless shirts and dresses that cover the bra strap and Timberlane sports jerseys."

A School-Wide Improvement Plan

Superintendent Earl F. Metzler 2d, who took over leadership of the Timberlane and Hampstead school systems Aug. 28 [2012], said the dress code was drafted by the high school's climate committee, a body that was formed over the summer to improve the learning environment in the building.

In addition to updating the school's dress code, the committee also adopted a new attendance policy, School Board members said.

The high school, which serves the communities of Atkinson, Danville, Plaistow, and Sandown [in New Hampshire], has been identified as a "school in need of improvement" for failing to meet federal benchmarks for student performance on the New England Common Assessment Program exam [a series of exams

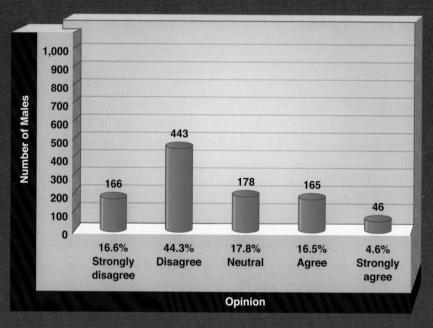

Are Sleeveless Shirts or Dresses Immodest?

In an online "Modesty Survey" of self-identified Christian males aged twelve and over, conducted by the Rebelution, only about 21 percent agreed that shirts and dresses revealing bare arms are immodest.

Taken from: The Rebelution. "Modesty Survey," 2007. http://therebelution.com/modestysurvey/browse.

that determine whether students are performing at grade level in core subjects].

The goal of the new policies was to make the school's expectations clear, Metzler said. According to Timberlane Regional School Board chairman Robert Collins, a Danville resident who has been on the board since 2008, the previous dress code included vague language that made enforcement difficult.

Under the new policy on proper attire, all students are "required to wear tops . . . that have sleeves, a modest neckline . . . and that are long enough to cover beyond their waist. The length of shorts, skirts, or dresses maybe no shorter than mid-thigh."

Students who violate the dress code are asked to change their clothing and may face disciplinary action, including detention and administrative probation, according to Timberlane's student handbook. Skerry and her supporters like to point out that many female role models—including [First Lady] Michelle Obama, British actress and humanitarian Audrey Hepburn, and singer-songwriter Taylor Swift—often favor sleeveless fashions.

"If the first lady can show her shoulders, my daughters can too," wrote Sandy Desmond, a follower of the Facebook page. "This is not acceptable! The school should focus more on empowering our daughters to be strong, intelligent, and independant [sic]," she wrote.

A Student Speaks Up

Skerry, a junior nicknamed Bitsy who is serving her third year as secretary for the class of 2014, has attracted national attention as news outlets as far away as California report on her campaign. One woman from nearby Kingston, N.H., said she was so impressed by Skerry that she named her pet chicken Bitsy, after the English honor society student.

But at Timberlane, Metzler said there has been an outpouring of support for a dress code.

"Many students and parents appreciate that we're making it clear that we have high expectations," he said.

There have been few violations of the dress code and no harsh disciplinary actions have been necessary, he said.

After Skerry addressed the School Board, Metzler asked Woodworth to reconvene the climate committee to review the new dress code—this time, with student input.

"I was very impressed with Bitsy's presentation," Metzler said. "She exercised her right to voice her opinion in a very respectful manner. I want to encourage student involvement, not just at the high school, but at all schools."

The climate committee met on Oct. 4 [2012] with Skerry and members of the high school's student council and peer outreach program. Although Skerry suggested school officials conduct a student survey to assess the impact of the dress code, no decisions regarding the policy were made at that meeting. The committee continues to examine the mandate, according to school officials.

"Dress codes define the basic standards for the community, not to control the students but to promote safe and productive learning environments," said Mark V. Joyce, executive director of the New Hampshire School Administrators Association, an organization that represents more than 300 school system leaders, including superintendents, assistant superintendents, and finance directors.

"Every decade has had its challenges," Joyce said, recalling the mini-skirts of the 1960s. "It's up to each individual community

Elizabeth Skerry, shown here wearing a cap-sleeve blouse, challenged her school officials about the dress code that prohibits sleeveless clothes at Timberlane Regional High School in Plaistow, New Hampshire. Her actions prompted a review of the policy by the school district superintendent.

to decide what is acceptable. In this case, student concerns are being considered by the administration. They are reviewing the matter. We just need to wait."

Her Head Held High

As the climate committee conducts its review, Skerry and her family are weighing their options, including legal action. The new policy, they said, targets female students disproportionately and sends students the wrong message—that girls who bare their shoulders are somehow "bad."

"It is a form of discrimination and gender bias," said Skerry, who has a passion for public speaking and plans to be a lawyer.

Her family is behind her 100 percent, said her father, Paul.

"If the policy isn't amended, we feel she should move forward with it and see this through," he said.

"When the media attention dies down, which it will, Bitsy's ultimately the one who will have to live with the decision she made to bring this issue out into the open," said her mother, Natalie. "I am so proud of her for speaking up for something she believes in. That's hard for many adults to do."

"Bitsy can walk into Timberlane High School with her head held high, knowing that no matter what the outcome, she stood for something—and her voice was heard."

What You Should Know About Dress Codes in Schools

Opinions About Dress Codes

Responding to a 2013 survey of 1,350 seventh and eighth graders whose schools had recently adopted uniforms, conducted by researchers from the University of Nevada–Reno College of Education:

- Ninety percent said that they did not like wearing uniforms.
- Fifty-four percent agreed or strongly agreed with the statement "I still have my identity when I wear a uniform."
- Fifty-three percent agreed or strongly agreed with the statement "My family likes that I wear a uniform to school."
- Fifty percent agreed or strongly agreed with the statement "I think uniforms save money on clothes."
- Forty-two percent agreed or strongly agreed with the statement "I worry less about how others look."
- Forty-one percent agreed or strongly agreed with the statement "There is less gang activity at school."

In June 2013 the National Association of Elementary School Principals partnered with retailer Lands' End to survey 517 principals and other school leaders. According to the survey, many leaders who have a school uniform policy or dress code at their school reported that their current policy has made a "significant, positive impact" on the following problems:

- Peer pressure (86 percent)
- Bullying (64 percent)

In the same survey principals reported that their current uniform or dress code policy has "made a positive impact" on several issues:

- Classroom discipline (85 percent)
- Image in the community (83 percent)
- Student safety (79 percent)
- School pride (77 percent)
- Student achievement (64 percent)
- Attendance (44 percent)

According to on-air polls about dress codes conducted by radio station WKDQ of Kentucky and Indiana in 2012:

- When asked whether school uniforms infringe on students' rights, 61.11 percent of respondents said, "No, schools have every right to require uniforms"; 25 percent said, "Yes, what about your right to choose and express yourself?"; 11.11 percent said, "A dress code that is adhered to would be a better option"; and 2.78 percent said, "Why is this even an issue?"
- Asked whether there should be a dress code for teachers, 62.07 percent said, "Yes"; 24.14 percent said, "As long as the boundaries are clearly defined"; 7 percent said, "There shouldn't be dress codes at all"; and 6.9 percent said, "No."

The Courts and Dress Codes in School

The US Supreme Court has never ruled specifically on dress codes in public schools but has ruled on important cases establishing or limiting students' rights to expression:

- *Tinker v. Des Moines Independent Community School District* (1969) defined the First Amendment rights of students in public schools. The court ruled that a school could not forbid students from wearing black armbands to protest the Vietnam War simply because administrators feared the armbands might be distracting. In the majority decision, Justice Abe Fortas famously wrote, "It can hardly be argued that either students or teachers shed their constitutional rights to freedom of speech or expression at the schoolhouse gate."

- *Bethel School District v. Fraser* (1986) affirmed that vulgar or lewd expression is not consistent with the "fundamental values" of public school education. The case concerned a student who was suspended for using graphic sexual references in a speech at school. The court ruled that school boards have the authority to determine when expression in the classroom or at school events is inappropriate.
- *Morse v. Frederick* (2007) ruled that schools may prohibit student expression in certain circumstances. The case involved a student at a school event who wore a T-shirt bearing a message that administrators interpreted as promoting the use of illegal drugs.

Lower courts have ruled on student attire and dress codes:
- *Olesen v. Board of Education of School District No. 228* (Northern District of Illinois, 1987) ruled that a school may ban male students from wearing earrings, because the jewelry does not convey any message protected by the First Amendment. The school still must demonstrate a legitimate academic purpose for banning the earrings.
- *Stephenson v. Davenport Community School District* (Eighth Circuit Court of Appeals, 1997) found that a school dress code that prohibited "gang colors, symbols, signals, signs" and "gang related activities" was too vague to be constitutional. A policy must have clear definitions for terms like *gang* or *gang activities*, the court ruled, so that those who attempt to follow the policy and those who must enforce it have clear guidance.
- *Phillips v. Anderson County School District* (District of South Carolina, 1997) ruled that a school had the right to suspend a student for wearing a jacket bearing the Confederate flag, because the school had a history of racial conflicts over the flag. In this case the student's right to expression was overruled by the school's responsibility to support an atmosphere conducive to education.
- *Chambers v. Babbitt* (District of Minnesota, 2001) upheld a student's First Amendment right to wear a shirt reading

"Straight Pride." The court acknowledged that the message might be hurtful to some viewers but found that the school had not demonstrated that a "substantial disruption" was likely to occur.

- *Palmer v. Waxahachie Independent School District* (Fifth Circuit Court of Appeals, 2009) upheld a Texas school's dress code that prohibits shirts with any non-school-related messages on them. The student in the case was disciplined for wearing a shirt with "Freedom of Speech" written on the front and the text of the First Amendment on the back. The court ruled that the school's policy was content-neutral and fair for everyone. In 2010 the US Supreme Court declined to rule on the case, letting the appeals court ruling stand.

Dress Codes in Other Countries

Virtually all high school students in public and private schools are required to wear uniforms in many countries, including:

- Australia
- Burma
- Cambodia
- China
- Ghana
- Indonesia
- Japan
- Nigeria
- Singapore
- South Africa
- Venezuela

What You Should Do About Dress Codes in Schools

When they learn that their school has adopted a new dress code or has started to require students to wear uniforms, many students are disappointed, even angry. The image of passive clones walking silently through the hallways like something out of a science-fiction movie comes to mind, and some students wonder how they can make themselves stand out when everyone looks the same. But most people get used to it, and many even come to like it. After all, members of a sports team or the military wear the same clothes, and for them, putting on the uniform makes them feel as though they truly belong to the team.

It will probably not be any comfort when well-meaning adults point out, "It's only for a few hours each day. You can wear what you want before and after school." After all, you spend a lot of time with those people at school—with your friends, your frenemies, and people you would like to impress. In terms of making a statement about who you are, the hours at school are important. But do consider whether the style you are trying to put on is really your own. If you wear a shirt that everyone has seen on television, in a movie, on the Internet, and in a commercial, does it really say anything about you as an individual? When you follow the latest trend, what are you saying about yourself?

Many students who attend schools with strict dress codes still find creative ways to express their own personalities. If your school has a typical dress code, you will have some restrictions (such as no bare arms, no exposed midriffs or underwear) but a lot of leeway. Look over your school's dress code carefully, focusing on what is allowed instead of what is not. You will probably see that you still have a lot of choices. As more schools adopt dress codes, many stores and designers are emphasizing styles that are school appropriate. If your school has a uniform, your shirt, pants, or skirt will be a lot like everyone else's. You may be able to highlight your individual style with little things: a piece of jewelry, a headband, a hairstyle, a belt, a tie, an unusual pair of socks. If these are not allowed, think about what you could do to make your backpack unique, or carry distinctive notebooks or pens.

Keep in mind that an important word in many school dress codes and related court cases is *distracting*. Teachers and administrators want your focus to be on learning while you are in school. So if you are wearing something to attract other students' attention, you are doing exactly what they do not want you to do—you are drawing other people's attention away from the lessons of the day. See it from their point of view, and you will save yourself the hassle of having to turn your shirt inside out, hand over the notebook with the bumper sticker on it, or wear the hideous sweater they keep in the principal's office for kids who show too much skin.

But if you have a strong opinion about whether or not your school should adopt a dress code or require students to wear uniforms, make sure you take advantage of opportunities to express that opinion. Most school systems make decisions about dress codes only after careful deliberation, and many conduct surveys of students, parents, or faculty and staff members before writing new rules about student attire. If your school's principal, superintendent, or board of education distributes a survey to students, make sure you fill it out and encourage others to do the same. If your school administrators make a decision without input from the community, you might ask those in charge to consider sending out a survey. There are many examples of these surveys on the Internet, posted by schools across the country. You could also prepare a presentation for your school's parent-teacher organization or your district's school board; many of these groups set aside time in their meetings for comments from the public. And if your school has a newspaper, wiki, or blog, you could write an editorial to explain your position.

There have been cases when students chose to deliberately violate their school dress code or uniform policy in order to express their opposition to it. Before you consider an action like this, you should know that the courts have generally ruled that public schools have the right to place reasonable restrictions on what students wear to school and that private schools have even broader powers to require or forbid student clothing. You should only decide to deliberately flout the rules about dress if you are willing to face the consequences, which could be severe—as severe as suspension or even expulsion from school. Probably it would be better to use your strong opinion about dress codes as an opportunity to practice your skills at gathering information and presenting it persuasively through effective writing and speaking.

Like many issues that come up at school, students and administrators see dress codes differently. Administrators generally adopt dress codes because they want to help students succeed and because they believe uniforms keep students safer, less distracted, and less interested in unhealthy materialistic competition. Students make good points when they ask for the opportunities to make their own choices—maybe even the right to learn from bad choices—or for modest accommodations like casual Fridays or spirit days. Like many issues that come up at school, dress codes provide opportunities for students, teachers, and administrators to engage in spirited, informed, respectful debate if both sides show a willingness to work together to find good solutions.

ORGANIZATIONS TO CONTACT

The editors have compiled the following list of organizations concerned with the issues debated in this book. The descriptions are derived from materials provided by the organizations. All have publications or information available for interested readers. The list was compiled on the date of publication of the present volume; names, addresses, phone and fax numbers, and e-mail and Internet addresses may change. Be aware that many organizations take several weeks or longer to respond to inquiries, so allow as much time as possible.

American Civil Liberties Union (ACLU)
125 Broad St., 18th Fl.
New York, NY 10004
website: www.aclu.org

Founded in 1920, the ACLU is a nonprofit and nonpartisan organization of more than five hundred thousand members and supporters. The mission of the ACLU is to preserve all of the protections and guarantees of the US Constitution's Bill of Rights. The group handles nearly six thousand court cases annually from offices in almost every state. The website has a collection of news articles, as well as a blog, news feeds, and podcasts. A page titled "Your Right to Free Expression" addresses students' concerns, including school attire. Recent news articles on the site include "Schools in Texas Routinely Violate Constitutional Protections for Religious Freedom" and "ACLU Expresses Concern Over Cleveland Schools' Plan to End Assistance to Families Who Cannot Afford Uniforms."

Anti-Defamation League (ADL)
605 Third Ave.
New York, NY 10158
(212) 885-7700
website: www.adl.org

The ADL was founded in 1913 to ensure justice and fair treatment for Jewish people and others. Now the nation's premier civil rights/human relations agency, the ADL fights anti-Semitism and all forms of bigotry, defends democratic ideals, and protects civil rights for all. Publications on the website include "Religion in the Public Schools: Dress Codes," "Religious Accommodation in the Workplace: Your Rights and Obligations."

First Amendment Center
John Seigenthaler Center at Vanderbilt University
1207 Eighteenth Ave. S.
Nashville, TN 37212
(615) 727-1600
e-mail: info@fac.org
website: www.firstamendmentcenter.org

The First Amendment Center supports the First Amendment and builds understanding of its core freedoms through education, information, and entertainment. The center is nonpartisan and does not lobby or litigate. Its website, one of the most authoritative sources of news, information, and commentary in the nation on First Amendment issues, features daily updates on news about First Amendment–related developments, including several stories about students and other citizens facing conflicts because of dress codes. There is also detailed information about US Supreme Court cases involving the First Amendment and commentary, analysis, and special reports involving free expression.

National Association of Elementary School Principals (NAESP)
1615 Duke St.
Alexandria VA 22314
(800) 386-2377 or (703) 684-3345
e-mail: naesp@naesp.oeg
website: www.naesp.org

Founded in 1921, the NAESP leads in advocacy and support for elementary and middle-level principals and other education leaders in their commitment to all children. The organization provides information, support, and legal advice for kindergarten through grade eight principals. The NAESP publishes the *Communicator* and *Principal* magazines and several newsletters. The website's "Legal Issues" page offers advice about topics such as dress codes and freedom of expression.

National Association of Secondary School Principals (NASSP)
1904 Association Dr.
Reston, VA 20191-1537
(703) 860-0200
website: www.principals.org

In existence since 1916, the NASSP is the preeminent organization of middle-level and high school principals, assistant principals, and aspiring school leaders from across the United States and more than forty-five countries around the world. The mission of the NASSP is to promote excellence in school leadership. Publications available on the website include the article "Student Dress: How Low Can It Go?" and the report "Expression Rights of Public School Employees and Students."

National Center for Education Statistics (NCES)
1990 K St. NW
Washington, DC 20006
(202) 502-7300
website: www.nces.org

The NCES is the primary federal entity for collecting and analyzing data related to education in the United States and other nations. The NCES is located within the US Department of Education and the Institute of Education Sciences. The center collects data from many sources covering all areas of education, including elementary and secondary education, postsecondary education, and international assessments. The website provides a massive collection of reports, fact sheets, and other publications for general readers, as well as databases and other tools for use by researchers. Information about how many schools require uniforms and dress codes is found in reports on the annual Crime and Safety Surveys.

National Education Association (NEA)
1201 Sixteenth St. NW
Washington, DC 20036-3290
(202) 833-4000
website: www.nea.org

The NEA, the nation's largest professional employee organization, is committed to advancing the cause of public education. The association's 3 million members work at every level of education—from preschool to university graduate programs. The NEA has affiliate organizations in every state and in more than fourteen thousand communities across the United States. Its website includes articles and reports on student and teacher rights, as well as debates on topics such as whether students should be suspended for inappropriate dress and whether teachers should wear business attire to school.

Working to Improve Schools and Education (WISE)
School of Humanities and Sciences
201 Muller Center
Ithaca College
Ithaca, NY 14850
(607) 274-3102
website: www.ithaca.edu/wise

WISE is a project of Ithaca College in Ithaca, New York. Its website is intended to provide anyone interested in improving US schools with valuable information and resources about important issues in education and teaching, with particular emphasis on issues of equity, diversity, multicultural education, and the development of schools that are more effective for all students and families. The group maintains a "School Uniforms" page with links to articles, statistics, and other websites.

Books

David L. Brunsma, *School Uniform Movement and What It Tells Us About American Education*. Lanham, MD: ScarecrowEducation, 2004.

David L. Brunsma, *Uniforms in Public Schools: A Decade of Research and Debate*. Lanham, MD: Rowman & Littlefield Education, 2006.

Suzanne Eckes and Charles J. Russo, *School Discipline and Safety*. Thousand Oaks, CA: Sage, 2012.

Roman Espejo, *Teen Rights and Freedoms: Dress*. Detroit: Greenhaven, 2012.

Dianne Gereluk, *Symbolic Clothing in Schools*. New York: Continuum, 2008.

Parme P. Giuntini and Kathryn Hagen, eds., *Garb: A Fashion and Culture Reader*. Saddle River, NJ: Prentice Hall, 2008.

David L. Hudson, *Let the Students Speak! A History of the Fight for Free Expression in American Schools*. Boston: Beacon, 2011.

Joseph G. Kosciw, et al., *The 2011 National School Climate Survey: The Experience of Lesbian, Gay, Bisexual and Transgender Youth in Our Nation's Schools*. New York: Gay, Lesbian and Straight Education Network, 2012.

Fiona MacDonald, *Uniforms Through History*. Milwaukee, WI: Gareth Stevens, 2007.

Ruthann Robson, *Dressing Constitutionally: Hierarchy, Sexuality, and Democracy from Our Hairstyles to Our Shoes*. New York: Cambridge University Press, 2013.

Philip D. Vairo, Sheldon Marcus, and Max Weiner, *Hot-Button Issues for Teachers: What Every Educator Needs to Know About Leadership, Testing, Textbooks, Vouchers, and More*. Lanham, MD: Rowman & Littlefield Education, 2007.

Periodicals and Internet Sources

Al Baker and Eric P. Newcomer, "Baring Shoulders and Knees, Students Protest a Dress Code," *New York Times*, June 7, 2012.

Wayne M. Barrett, "Uniform Appeal," *USA Today*, May 1, 2010.

Thomas Bartlett, "Black Colleges React to Low Point in Fashion," *Chronicle of Higher Education*, November 8, 2009.

Greg Beato, "I'm with Stupid: Message T-shirts," *Reason*, April 2008.

Marsha Boutelle, "Uniforms: Are They a Good Fit?," *Education Digest*, February 2008.

Marc Brasof, "Student Input Improves Behavior, Fosters Leadership," *Phi Delta Kappan*, October 2011.

Alexis Brindley and Peter Brosnan, "What Not to Wear: A School's Dress Code Limits Clothing Styles and Colors," *Current Events*, March 28, 2011.

Steven M. Brown and Howard J. Bultinck, "From Black Armbands to Bong Hits for Jesus: The 40th Anniversary of *Tinker*," *Phi Delta Kappan*, June 2009.

Matt Buesing, "Dress Code Adoption: A Year's Worth of Steps," *School Administrator*, April 2011.

Kevin Chappell, "A Modern Morehouse Man," *Ebony*, September 2010.

Stephanie Clifford and Karen Ann Cullotta, "A Little Give in the Dress Code," *New York Times*, September 2, 2011.

David Coleman, "Civilizing the Pack Mentality," *New York Times*, September 15, 2011.

Gail Collins, "More Guns, Fewer Hoodies," *New York Times*, March 29, 2012.

K.J. Dell'Antonio, "You're Not Wearing That to School," *New York Times*, September 9, 2012.

Education World, "Dressing (Teachers) for Success," 2012. www.educationworld.com/a_admin/admin/admin422_a.shtml.

Ashley Gatewood, "Hats for Better Health," *Americas*, July–August 2010.

John A. Gavin, "Dress Codes a Success," *Record* (Bergen County, NJ), February 8, 2011.

Marion Herbert, "Dressing for Class with Class," *District Administrator*, March 2012.

Jan Hoffman, "Can a Boy Wear a Skirt to School?," *New York Times*, November 6, 2009.

Reynolds Holding, "Speaking Up for Themselves: Freedom of Speech in Schools," *Time*, May 21, 2007.

Sabrina James, "Rock That School Uniform!," *Parenting School Years*, October 9, 2012.

Bonnie A. Kellman, "Tinkering with Tinker: Protecting the First Amendment in Public Schools," *Notre Dame Law Review*, November 2009.

Jessica Lahey, "A Dress-Code Enforcer's Struggle for the Soul of the Middle-School Girl," *Atlantic*, February 2013.

Amanda Marcotte, "If You Don't Want Girls Judged by Their Hemlines, Stop Judging Them by Their Hemlines," *Slate*, February 15, 2013. www.slate.com/blogs/xx_factor/2013/02/15 /dress_codes_for_girls_they_don_t_teach_self_respect_only _respecting_girls.html.

Iris Pagan, "Hoodies and the School Dress Code," Examiner .com, April 2, 2012. www.examiner.com/article/hoodies-and -the-school-dress-code.

Andrew Potter, "What's Beneath That Ban on Baggy Pants?," *Maclean's*, September 10–17, 2007.

Rebecca Raby, "'Tank Tops Are OK but I Don't Want to See Her Thong': Girls' Engagement with Secondary School Dress Codes," *Youth & Society*, March 2010.

Bonnie Rochman, "Banning the Bandz," *Time*, June 14, 2010.

Marinda Valenti, "What Do Dress Codes Say About Girls' Bodies?," *Ms.*, May 24, 2013. http://msmagazine.com /blog/2013/05/24/what-do-dress-codes-say-about-girls-bodies.

Laurence M. Vance, "Dress Codes and a Free Society," *Explore Freedom*, May 1, 2013.

Angela Walmsley, "What the United Kingdom Can Teach the United States About School Uniforms," *Phi Delta Kappan*, March 2011.

INDEX